The Advanc

Collection:

3 Books in 1 Bundle

How to Improve Your Spoken English Fast

English Fluency For Advanced English Speaker

Accent Reduction for Professionals

Public Speaking Secrets

Whitney Nelson

English Fluency For Advanced English Speaker

How to Unlock The Full Potential to Speak English Fluently

Advanced Edition

Whitney Nelson

Contents

Introduction

Congratulations! You're already an advanced student of the English language. Before you take another step in your journey of learning, though, you need to pause a moment and celebrate your success thus far.

English is no easy language to learn. It's filled with idioms that make no literal sense and colloquialisms that you may only hear once in a blue moon (like the phrase I just used). If that weren't enough, there are hundreds (if not thousands) of exceptions to the established rules of grammar – especially when it comes to turning single nouns into plural nouns. The plural of alumnus is alumni, but the plural of campus is campuses. And there's really no rule you can memorize to know that except to memorize them initially. After you speak it for a while, then you get to know almost intuitively.

But you already know the challenges that face you. I'm sure you've already been swamped with many of these puzzling contradictions already. Despite all those obstacles, though, you've progressed this far, successfully encountering every twist and turn the language has thrown at you.

But, you've encountered a problem you just can't seem to solve. You've reached a plateau in your fluency. Sure, you can read the language and understand it fairly well when it's spoken quickly by native speakers. Nothing you do, however, seems to help you to make any more progress. In a phrase: you're stuck.

Stop it right there. You hear other students speak the language well. Your first thought is "Why can't I do that?"

Ahh, but you can. That's why I've written this book. It's created just for you – the advanced English student who desires to take his/her ability to speak the language to the next level.

Don't believe me?

What if I told you that armed with seven well-kept secrets you can nearly effortlessly soar to the next level of fluency in your study of English? All the struggling you've done, all the doubts you've had will fade away once your ability to speak the language you're so excited about using improves.

How can I be so sure that these steps will work? Because not only have I used them, but thousands of others have used these same techniques to improve their skills and crack through that glass ceiling. I started sharing these secrets with interested friends, family, and students. Today, they're speaking like English was their native tongue.

And you, too, can be among those successful students who discover the joy of conquering a language they once thought impossible to learn.

This Book is Not for Beginners

This book provides you with the key secrets you'll need to unlock the next level of fluency and open an entirely new world of fluency. With this book by your side, you'll discover that taking your skills to the next level wasn't nearly as difficult as you originally imagined it to be.

In this book, you'll not only discover the secrets, but you'll also find the encouragement to continue in your studies. As you read these pages, you'll feel as if you have your own personal English tutor sitting right next to you, guiding you every step of the way.

Having been in the same position myself at one time and helping hundreds of others in this identical situation, I have a good idea of what's running through your mind as we go through these steps.

The content of the book is arranged so that the first chapters have a general wide appeal and will help just about everyone become better at the spoken word. As you read farther in the book each section talks about the language in a bit more success. This doesn't mean that you can't understand Chapter Two without reading Chapter One. Feel free to read these chapters in any order, based on your perceived personal needs.

In the first chapter, we'll review the five myths about English that are the common obstacles of most students. You'll undoubtedly recognize at least one of them as an impediment to your learning. Once you know the myth or myths holding you back, it'll just be a matter of time to change your thinking and continue studying.

The following chapter introduces you to an effective method of creating attainable goals for yourself. Called S.M.A.R.T. goals, you'll learn how even a minimum of planning can bring a maximum of learning. You'll want to not waste a single minute implementing them in your learning schedule. Guaranteed. Not only will this goal-setting technique help you in pursuit of learning to speak the English language, but you can transfer these goal-setting skills to any dream you'd like to manifest.

The third secret to fluency is to immerse yourself in the language. Easier said than done, you say? Most students mistakenly believe that the only way to do that is to travel to meet native speakers. That's why the chapter is filled tips that'll have yourself "swimming" in English before you realize it.

None of these guidelines require travel or even walking up to total strangers and starting conversations. In fact, they all involve low-risk situations that will have you speaking English in safe, low-risk situations more often than you ever thought possible.

When you begin reading chapter four's secret to success, you may shake your head in disbelief, but by the time you've finished it you'll be eager and excited to implement suggestions. That's because this involves the one step most of us fear most when we're learning anything, not just the English language. The secret key: it's perfectly fine to make mistakes. In fact, it's not only perfectly fine, but it's nearly mandatory. It's guaranteed to change your entire way of viewing the learning process.

What does listening have to do with speaking a language? Everything! In the fifth step, you'll not only discover how improving this one habit can improve your fluency by leaps and bounds. The chapter also provides you with techniques to develop your active listening skills and then translate those into the breakthrough in your speaking of English.

But that's not all, we take listening to new heights with a technique called "extensive listening." Discover how it can be the key to your breakthrough in propelling you into new English-speaking opportunities.

Then we move on to the next chapter in which you'll learn about one of the most effective methods of learning any language. Known in academic circles as shadowing, this method is also called parroting by those who use it often. Essentially, you'll be improving your fluency the way you learned your native language.

In this technique, you'll be repeating the sounds of those speaking English word for word almost at the same time the person is speaking. You'll learn how you can use this technique in a variety of situations. With today's technology, shadowing is easier than ever before.

Your Journey to Fluency

While this volume is meant to be a student's guidebook through the English language, it's really so much more. You'll find yourself referring to this book again and again in your journey of learning.

Are you prepared to climb to new levels of fluency nearly effortlessly? It's time to discover what's been keeping you on this plateau of learning. It's time to remove the obstacles in your path and seriously continue on this amazing path of learning you've set your sights on.

Let's get started!

Chapter 1: *Getting Over the Plateau to Become a Fluent English Speaker*

Are you frustrated? Do you believe you've hit the peak of your learning with regard to the English language? You can read the language. You know the grammar and you can understand it when you hear the spoken word.

Yet, you're not speaking it as fluently as you want to – as you need to. No, there's nothing wrong with you. Many persons learning English feel as you do. They've reached a certain point in their ability to speak the language and just can't seem to advance any farther.

Unfortunately, they believe that what they've learned is all that they *can* learn. They've tried and tried to reach that next level fluency but to no avail.

Does this sound like your story? Are you ready to throw up your hands and give up, thinking any more progress is hopeless? Don't quit.

But before you continue any farther, stop knocking your head against the wall. Obviously what you're doing right now is not working. It's time to step back and analyze what needs to be changed in your approach to learning.

Instead of going any further in your pursuit of learning the spoken English language, you need to look into your own thinking to discover if you're holding any "limiting beliefs" holding you back. These are really myths that many people hold as the truth about their ability to learn to speak English fluently that, quite frankly, just aren't true.

Here are five of the most common limiting beliefs that students of English believe are natural barriers to their learning. These "beliefs" which many attributes to holding them back from being a more fluent speaker are really nothing more but preconceived notions. They can be overcome simply by changing your thinking. Then you can break that barrier to attain the next level of fluency. It may sound a bit strange, but it really does work.

5 Myths That May Be Hindering Your English Fluency

1. Your age

This is just an excuse. At one time scientists believed that as persons aged, the harder it was for them to learn. And not just the English language, everything – math, science even the adopting of new hobbies like knitting or playing the piano.

If you think about it, that's a pretty dismal diagnosis. The standard scientific thought stated that your brain cells continued to reproduce and were receptive to learning only up to a certain age. Once you reached that age your body would no longer make any new cells. If you could learn anything new, it would be much more difficult, taking a longer period of time. Whatever it was you wanted to learn, the scientists warned you it would be an uphill battle.

The lesson people took from this dictum? If you didn't learn a language when you were younger, well you were out of luck. You weren't about to learn it as an older individual. If you did manage it, you'd be struggling every step of the way.

Today, scientists have discovered that proclamation – taken as a law for so long – is not in the least bit true.

You need to know right now that your age doesn't limit your ability to speak English fluently. It's more likely you believing your age is a limiting factor actually keeps you from learning. Once you overcome this mindset, you'll discover that English isn't as difficult to speak as you thought – and before you know it you've unlocked the secret that has prevented you from going any further.

It's time to stop blaming your age for that plateau you've reached to learn and start using the English language more. With the suggestions presented throughout the rest of this book, you'll discover that it's easier than you once believed.

2. Fear of making mistakes.

Many individuals refuse to speak English as often as they could. Why? Simply because they're afraid of making mistakes. But worse than that they believe that someone will hear them make these mistakes and laugh at them.

The thought of making a mistake when speaking English shouldn't inhibit you or limit your speaking it in any way. In fact, it really should do the exact opposite – it should spur you on to speak it all the more.

Deep down you already know what I'm about to tell you: mistakes are your friends. Making a mistake when you talk is the ultimate way to learn the English language or any language for that matter.

Every single person learning a language made some type of mistake when they started. In fact, if the truth is known, they made what they considered more than their fair share of blunders. Even native speakers don't speak perfect English. Listen closely to some native speakers and you'll see exactly what I mean.

What if I told you that instead of fearing those mistakes, you should be embracing them? Would you think I was totally insane? Well, that's exactly what you should be doing – speaking more and making more mistakes. That's because the more mistakes you make, the faster you'll learn.

Let me tell you a story about two individuals, both learning English. Both, in fact, were at about the same level of fluency. They could read and comprehend English well and in general, had a good grasp of speaking it. Both wanted to go beyond where they were currently and hit the next level of fluency.

But one student feared speaking it, not only in her daily life but also in the classroom. She would never volunteer in class and when called upon she would barely speak up. When she did answer, she used as few words as possible. The instructor continually asked her to expand on her answers.

The other student, coincidentally, was in the same classroom and took every opportunity to speak English. He was the student always first to volunteer to answer in English. Instead of just answering with a short phrase or a one-word answer, he would make sure he'd elaborate a bit more – sometimes more than he needed to. The point is that he took every opportunity in class to speak English.

Not only that, but he would make sure he used the language as much as possible outside of the classroom as well. He made a concerted to associate with people who spoke English and made it a point to speak up in conversations even. If someone corrected his English, he thanked them. He would go on to explain that he was still learning and appreciated the corrections.

You could tell in an instant that the first student shied from talking because she feared to make mistakes. She believed that every word that came out of her mouth had to be perfect. The second student, though, approached his learning not only as a positive activity but something that was actually fun. Making mistakes didn't bother him.

You can guess who learned to speak English more quickly and more fluently. Don't let fear of making mistakes – either in class or in public – hold you back from speaking the language. We've all made mistakes – whether we're learning a language or math or any other subject. Mistakes are the foundation of any type of learning.

3. You can't remember all the rules of grammar.

Wow! Definitely, don't let this hold you back. No one, not even native speakers, can remember all the grammar rules. In fact, few speakers even try to follow all the rules. This includes native English speakers. If you took the time to review all the grammar that went into speaking a sentence before you spoke it, you'd never utter another English sentence.

Instead, place your faith in your vocabulary and especially listening to others. And if you make it a point to speak English, stop holding yourself to some impossible standard; you'll never ever enjoy the language. Believe it or not, learning a new language is fun – really fun.

Perfect grammar is the last thing you need to worry about. Instead, spend your time expanding your vocabulary, learning new words and using them as much as possible in conversations. Speak English every chance you get – whether you're clear about the grammar involved in the sentences you used or not.

This book is all about speaking the English language fluently. It's not about learning grammar. It's about using the language. Let's say that you're in a group of people and want to say that you ate an apple yesterday. If your grammar is shaky you may say "I yesterday apple eat."

Don't worry about making a fool of yourself. A native speaker may correct you and tell you the sentence is structured like this: "I ate an apple yesterday." Poof! You've learned to speak the language a little better through speaking up. And now you actually have a pattern for speaking a sentence like that.

You've learned first how to pattern a sentence in the past tense. You've also learned that the past tense of eat is "ate."

In that small insignificant mistake, you've broken through to the next level.

And the best part is that you didn't have to struggle over any grammar rules. All in all, you probably now feel better about yourself. Not only for speaking up but for actually learning how to use English grammar at the same time. Imagine how quickly you can improve your grammar without even thinking about it just by speaking a few sentences. Imagine what would happen if you spoke even more.

Instead of holding yourself up in your house and studying the dizzying array of grammar rules before you speak, get together with English speakers – native speakers and students like yourself – and use the vocabulary you've already learned.

4. You need to travel to be able to speak English fluently.

Another fallacy. You don't need to travel anywhere in order to improve your speech. There are many people who have learned the English language without going very far from home. If you're already living in the United States, that's not so much an issue, anyway.

But if you're currently living outside an English-speaking country and learning the language with an eye to visiting such a country in the near future you may view learning English is a hopeless pursuit. You may also be re-assessing why you're even bothering to learn the language.

Don't start second-guessing yourself. You can learn the language from wherever you are at the moment even if you don't have access to what you think you need. Have access to a computer? Then you already know how many video clips are on the web in English. Listen to these, repeat what these speakers say and the way they say it. Imagine these speakers are in the same room with you.

If you have to, stop the video and repeat what they've said, then double check yourself. There are plenty of ways of learning English – and as long as you're learning, there is no wrong way.

The key here is to focus on learning it using a method that's available for you. Instead of mourning that you can't travel or you don't know anyone who is speaking the language, dig around on the internet and find an English-speaking site. You may even discover a site that teaches you English. There are certainly plenty out there.

5. There are no other people around me speaking English.

This is a corollary to the "I can't travel to an English speaking country" myth. While it certainly would be easier if you know individuals who could speak English, it's definitely not essential – regardless of what you've heard to the contrary.

With a computer keyboard at your fingertips and the internet, it doesn't matter whether you live with or next door to English speakers or not. With less effort than you'd ever imagine on your part, you can find someone who speaks English.

Not only that, I'm betting that you'll also discover students of English – just like yourself – who are looking for others who speak at their level of fluency. Imagine how much you all could help each other. Imagine how much you can learn with only a bit of effort on your part.

These are the five most common complaints that people use to block their excelling at speaking the English language like a native. How many of these apply to you?

What Are Your Personal Myths?

Do you have any other personally limiting beliefs that hold you back from learning to speak the English language? If you do, why not stop right now and write them down. Now study them really well. Are those really valid reasons for not learning the English language? Can you think of any way you can overcome them?

Regardless of what your personal thoughts are about your inability to get to the next level of English fluency, remember that the only thing that is holding you back are your beliefs. The moment you believe you can learn to speak the English language like a native, you will.

It's time to think more positively about your ability to improve your ability to speak the English language. Just changing your thinking from "Wow! This is really difficult," to "Hey, this is getting easier all the time!" will help you speak more fluently. Guaranteed.

Chapter 2: Setting S.M.A.R.T. Goals -- The Secret of Getting What You Want When You Want It

Pedro complained to his English instructor one day that he was disappointed that his fluency in the language seemed to have hit a peak. "I can't advance any farther," he said, "and I'm far from sounding like a native speaker. And that is the long run is my goal. Did I set my sights too high?"

The instructor told him that, indeed, he did not set any goal that he could not accomplish; he just may have to re-think how to reach them. That's when he told Pedro about S.M.A.R.T. goals.

Are you feeling "stuck" in your level of learning? Are you, like Pedro, beginning to think you'll never break through to that next level of learning in which you sound more fluent – more like a native speaker?

Then perhaps it's time you look into using S.M.A.R.T. goals as well. What are they? What makes SMART goals different from any other? Simple. When you create this type of goal, you're strategically placing yourself in a position of achieving them. If you follow the guidelines of these techniques, in fact, it would be extremely difficult to fail.

S.M.A.R.T

I can hear you now, "When do we start?" Well, there's no time like the present. S.M.A.R.T. is an acronym for Specific, Measurable, Attainable, Responsible and Time-Bound. If you make your goals in accordance with these five guidelines, you're well on your way to fulfilling your English-language dreams.

But more than that, this is a technique used by a growing number of business executives as well as entrepreneurs to move their projects forward. It's time-tested. And the best part is that you can take these guidelines and use them for any goals you have for your life.

The letter "S" in S.M.A.R.T. stands for specific. You've probably created many goals in your life. Think back to several of them. Think about the times you succeeded as well as those instances in which you didn't reach them. What made the difference? What did you do right when you achieved your goals? How did this differ from the times you didn't reach your dreams?

Perhaps it could be that the ones you achieved were worded more specifically. Did you know exactly what you wanted? This works regardless of what your goals are—they aren't necessarily related to your learning the English language.

Take, for example, the individual who wanted to lose weight. She started out by saying that "someday" she'd like to lose weight. But until she decided specifically how many pounds she wanted to lose, her weight held steady. Once she made the decision and gave herself a deadline, however, she couldn't understand why she couldn't stick to an eating plan.

So your first step is deciding specifically what it is you want to do. Once you know exactly what it is, then create specific steps you believe will get you there. Let's say your goal is to be able to speak English well enough to make a presentation in front of your supervisors and several department managers at work.

Now write down what you believe you need to do in order to speak English well enough to do it. These are your steps for reaching your goals. For example, if giving a presentation is the goal, you must look critically at your spoken language skills now.

Decide what type of improvements you need to make. You may decide you

- Want to work on your pronunciation
- Learn more vocabulary words – as well as perfect their pronunciation
- Learn how to tell a joke in English

What else do you believe is keeping you from reaching this level of fluency in the English language. Not sure? Ask your instructor or a trusted friend.

Make sure you keep a list of these, because you'll need them for the next step. Keeping in mind your goal of making this presentation, we'll go to the next step in S.M.A.R.T. goals

The M in S.M.A.R.T. goals stands for measurable. That may be a no-brainer when it's said that way, but you'd be surprised how many people create goals without thinking about how they're going to measure their progress. And if you can't measure whether you're a quarter of the way to your goal or half to making your dream come true, how will you ever know when you've reached that particular goal?

That's why you need to discover a way to measure your progress. Let's continue with the example we used in the previous paragraphs. You want to perfect your ability to speak English so you can give a presentation at work.

The first thing we listed that needed to be improved was your ability to pronounce English.

Let's say this is your goal as well. Just saying it doesn't get it done. You could spend years perfecting it, but never recognize when your speech is, indeed, good enough. Your first decision – and creating a measurable goal – is to either recognize your improvement yourself or getting someone's opinion on your pronunciation. Ideally, this would be your instructor or a trusted friend.

You see how by adding this idea of measuring your improvement, you've created a goal you can work toward – and feel good about attaining once you've reached it.

Your second step in speaking English well enough to make a presentation was expanded your vocabulary. Here again, you need to set a certain number of words you want to learn and to pronounce. If you don't settle on how many words, you could be learning words forever. So not only settle on how many, but perhaps pick out a few from an English book, or ask your English teacher for recommendations on a few words. You may even want to ask a few colleagues what type of words they would recommend that may be business related.

Within this, you'll then want to start tackling this list. In addition to having friends and tutors help with your pronunciation, remember the web – especially any dictionary applications or sites you have access to. The definition each entry provides you with a proper pronunciation of the word.

And finally one of your goals was to be able to tell a joke. How are you going to turn this into a measurable goal? You may want to practice in front of the mirror or with a good friend who'll be honest with you. Once you've earned the thumbs of a friend you may want to take your joke to several more people to get their opinions.

The key to success in creating any successfully measurable goal is to look at the details of what needs to be done and honestly evaluate your ability to do it. Making the decision on how to measure your progress is a big step in ensuring this will work.

While you should never give up your dream, you also need to be open to the process of making it measurable as well as creating the best possible strategy to make this happen You also need to continually reassess how vital these goals are to you.

Now that you have one or more goals that are specific measurable, your next step is to ensure that your goals are attainable   Yes, the A in S.M.A.R.T. goals stand for attainable.

This is an important aspect of creating any goal – not just those related to your speaking English. This step may take some time. First, you need to be absolutely honest with yourself. What do you truly believe you can attain. Don't overstretch your reach and set some impossible goal that is beyond your level. That will only disappoint you and you may wrongly believe learning English is simply beyond your capability.

It's better to set a goal and break it into two steps and reach it than set one that's simply impossible to reach. Let's face it I'm five foot two inches tall. If my goal were to play professional basketball that may be seen as an unattainable goal. But to set a goal that I make so certain percentage of the shots I take on the court is attainable for me. That goal involves more my skill more than my natural height.

Pedro, for example, originally set a goal of learning how to pronounce fifteen new words a week. Before he committed himself to that goal, though, he thought long and hard if it really were attainable. Having second thoughts, he instead set his sights on learning ten – at least for the first week. After that, he would adjust his goal depending on how he performed the first week.

When you're working with the idea of whether your goals are attainable, you may have to be flexible. If you discover that you set your sights a bit too high, reduce them. There's no shame in doing that. In fact, having a desire that is at least realistic will help build your self-confidence.

On the other hand, you don't want to make your target so easy that it doesn't challenge you. If your goal is too easy, you won't push yourself to do your best – and you may even lose interest.

Pedro may also want to create an attainable goal that he can meet with a teacher or close friend weekly to help him with his speaking. Once a week, for example, sounds reasonable. If he set his sights on meeting with someone five times a week that may be a bit excessive and end up being something he couldn't achieve – which would possibly make him feel as if he failed. In reality, he really didn't fail, he simply underestimated the time involved in meetings like that.

Pedro gave much thought to how to perfect telling a joke and the attainability of that goal as well. He admired several comedians on television. The question he had to ask himself was should he hold himself up to a professional level of delivery when he wasn't even a native speaker.

The fact of the matter was that he admired the presentations of several of his colleagues who had told some great jokes. The attainable goal, then, would be to practice until he felt he could present more like them. He thought that would be an attainable goal.

He could learn to pitch these jokes through various ways – including professionals on television as well as the colleagues you work with. Pedro also recorded himself telling the joke to review his pronunciation.

Not only does Pedro have to learn to be flexible, he has to discover what smaller, equally attainable, goals he breaks this dream into smaller chunks.

The letter R in S.M.A.R.T. goals stands for the word responsible. The question becomes who is responsible for achieving this goal. The obvious answer is Pedro. As you create your goals, it will become quite apparent that you are ultimately responsible. What Pedro learned as he went along, however, as he needed to hold those who offered services of their help responsible as well.

He would have difficulty attaining some of the goals without the help of his friends, colleagues, and instructors. This by no means absolves him of all responsibility for achieving them, but it does mean he may have to endure in some of that those who offered to help him actually do.

If that should occur, he may have to take the imitative in reminding his instructor or others that they had volunteered to help. He may have to suggest times they could meet. Pedro can't – and neither can you – just ask for help and then expect them to always take the initiative to help you.

Other issues that may fall under the responsible portion of the S.M.A.R.T. goals include the amount of time you can realistically invest in each goal. Hold yourself responsible for ensuring you've created goals that overextend you or your resources. If you set unrealistic goals, you'll be disappointed and tempted to give up.

You'll also have to approach your goals responsibly. A large part of that is knowing when to ask for help. It could be that you need someone to spend time with you and assess your pronunciation. It could also be something as simple as an individual who you report to occasionally who holds you accountable for your progress.

The T of the acronym of S.M.A.R.T. represents the phrase time-bound. Have you ever heard the saying that goals without a deadline are dreams? While it's admirable to have dreams, the word itself implies that it's something that you'll see fulfilled in the future. Or worse yet something that's totally unachievable.

You're not dealing with pie-in-the-sky dreams that you don't expect to come true. Not by a long shot. You're creating specific targets that you expect to reach. When can you expect to see these goals manifest? That's up to you.

One thing is one hundred percent certain, though: if you don't hold yourself to a deadline, they'll never materialize. Pedro discovered this. He found that if he didn't put a specific time to reach his goal, he was far less likely to actually achieve them.

Pedro, for example, knew that it would take some time before he would be able to master the English language well enough to present a project report to his colleagues at work. So he set his sights on achieving them in one year.

But he also knew that he had to do the same thing with the intermediate goals that would eventually get him to his dream. So he sat down with pencil and a calendar in order to start assigning a timeline to his smaller goals.

In order to do this correctly, he needed to analyze the smaller goals and set an attainable timeline for all of his goals. The moment he realized that he would be running behind on one of the smaller aims, he then would need to re-evaluate all the goals which followed. It could mean that he would encounter a chain reaction. All the steps after that one would also be met later than he had intended.

If he encountered this, he could handle this is two ways. First, he could just delay the attainment of these steps and assignment himself a later manifestation day. Or, he could adjust his goals – even if it means working a bit harder and longer – in order to reach his ultimate goal on time.

The point of setting specific completion dates is that it helps you to plan. Pedro set a final target date for one year. A year from the day he started he hoped to be standing in front of his colleagues informing them about the progress of a project. If he saw he was falling behind on this timetable, he could then adjust his intermediate steps to recover some of the lost time.

Being held time-bound for a goal is also a great motivating factor to aid in your planning. Once Pedro set a final goal, he worked backward in planning deadlines for all the smaller steps. He started with his final goal date and carefully charted where he had a be a month before his final goal and then two months before that date.

He actually spent quite a bit of time figuring out how much time he'd need for all the smaller steps needed in order to get where he wanted to be on time.

Pedro decided that in a week he should work on one lesson on vocabulary – learning the meaning of the words. Additionally, he needed to put in two practice sessions on pronunciation. One of those would be conducted on his own with the help of a recorder and the internet and one would be – when possible – with his instructor or a good friend.

The final decision Pedro made in fulfilling the time-bound portion of the S.M.A.R.T. goals was to take a few moments periodically in order to assess his progress. He set his assessment dates as once a month. He compared where he was to where he hoped to be. Was he on track? Would he be able to make his goal within the time frame he set? Or was he running behind?

Did he need to increase the number of vocabulary words he was learning every week or did he need more work on his pronunciation? Whatever he eventually decided, he fine-tuned his schedule to accommodate his ultimate completion date.

S.M.A.R.T goals are an excellent method of ensuring you don't lose sight of your desires. How many times have set New Year's resolutions only to find by February, you realize you're not working toward them? That's because you didn't apply the follow-up work necessary to keep you laser-focused on your goal. You merely wrote down some vague goal and went on with your life. Your New Year's resolutions become nothing more than afterthoughts as you continued on with your life.

You can easily see how setting – and maintaining – S.M.A.R.T. goals are essential in manifesting your desire to speak English fluently. The key to working these goals is to keep them uppermost in your mind. Pedro learned – and so you'll discover this as well – that learning English is a daily discipline. You can't learn to speak fluently by cramming a week's worth of work into a day or two.

The Need for Flexibility

The other lesson Pedro learned from instituting this technique is that he needed to maintain a degree of flexibility. If a step isn't working, then he needed to revise it. If he hadn't progressed as far as he had hoped by the end of a month or so, he needed to re-assess his strategy. He needed to analyze what was working and what wasn't. and he needed to do it on a regular basis.

But there is one more action Pedro took when he successfully completed each of his smaller goals. He rewarded himself. At the very least, he stopped for a few moments and told himself how good he was doing. Sometimes, he would treat himself to a dinner out or buy himself a small present.

You should consider doing something similar. It needn't be a large purchase or even a huge dinner. The important thing is that you stop for several moments and compliment yourself on doing a good job. Then cheer yourself on to going all the way.

Once you've set your goals, it's time to move on to learning methods on achieving these goals. In the next chapter, you'll learn that the fastest way to learn English is to just dive into the language. You'll also learn some techniques for doing just that.

Chapter 3: Immerse Yourself in the English Language

Have you ever wondered what the difference is between an individual who seems to glide through learning the English language and someone who struggles with every word – perhaps even every syllable?

You may have assumed that's it a matter of skill. You dismiss their success as a natural talent they possess for learning the spoken word. You may even credit them with being smarter than the average person.

Well, you may think all of that, but you'd be wrong. Those who learn how to speak English fluently are neither smarter than you nor do they necessarily have a gift for learning languages.

What separates those who learn the spoken word of English from those who don't can be described in one word: immersion.

What? Those who seem to learn effortlessly simply immerse themselves in the language. They seek out opportunities to speak English at every turn. If they have to make a choice between speaking their native language or English, they choose English every chance they get.

Consider this for a moment. You'll never improve at any activity – jogging, playing piano or even knitting – unless you practice. Practicing the English language is the only way to immerse yourself in the language.

The Only Way to Learn English

Believe it or not, you can be the person who others envy at your quick grasp of the English language. You can be the individual who speaks it with ease. And you can start right now. As long as you keep these guidelines in mind.

1. Don't spend a lot of time perfecting your grammar.

Believe it or not, this is probably *the most important rule in learning how to speak English.*

Your goal isn't to write a paragraph in English with no grammatical mistakes. Your goal is to speak it. So don't obsess about grammar. If you listen closely to native speakers not everyone speaks English perfect all the time.

Let's face it, at this point in your studies you already have a firm grasp of English grammar. You probably could even correct a native speaker when they don't use proper grammar. So, if your goal is to become a better speaker you need to focus on using it as if it were your first language.

Actually, studying grammar will only hinder your development using the spoken word. If you analyze what you're about to say and think about all the grammar rules before you speak, you'll discover the precise moment to say what you wanted to.

When you're thinking about this guideline you need to know that even most native speakers of the English language only know about 20 percent of all the hundreds (and hundreds) of the rules. A mere 20 percent. At this point in your studies, you probably already know more than that.

Don't worry, the more frequently you speak English, you'll undoubtedly get an ear for proper grammar. After a while, the sound of an improperly structured sentence or verbs that don't agree with your subject will sound horrible. As long as you know what sounds right, you'll be able to speak it well enough. I'm guessing that, as an advanced student, you already have a grasp of this aspect of your learning.

2. Learn phrases, not words.

Think about it. You probably know many vocabulary words. And you undoubtedly know how to pronounce them. But what you really need to study at this point are phrases. While knowing the words are, indeed, important, languages are really a compilation of phrases.

I'm sure you know students of the language who have an impeccable grasp of vocabulary words but still can't create a sentence if their life depended on it. Why? They failed to study English phrases.

When children learn how to talk, they're definitely immersed in their native language. It's usually the only language they hear from the moment they wake up until they're tucked into bed at night. What they hear are not separate words, but sentences, phrases and everything in between.

If you already know about 1,000 words (and you probably know more than that right now), you could still find yourself stumbling over stringing more than two sentences together to engage yourself intelligently in conversation.

But all you really need to know is approximately 100 phrases and you'll be able to string sentence after sentence with ease. In contrast, you'll be surprised how much more fluent you'll be. If you know 1,000 separate words, you may be able to correctly create one sentence. Only one sentence.

If you learn 100 phrases you'll be able to speak many more sentences. And if you get ambitious and learn 1,000 phrases (it's not nearly as difficult as it seems) . . . well . . . you'll be nearly as fluent as a native speaker.

Once you learn even a few of these phrases a week, your understanding of speaking this language with exploding exponentially. The trick is to learn the phrase so well that you only have to exert a small amount effort on completing them.

Listed below are several of the most common phrases in the language. How many of them do you know? If you find there are some you're stumbling over, then you may want to study those some.

- *How often do you (plus verb)?*
- *Can I help you (plus verb or as a question by itself)?*
- *It's too late for that*
- *You could have (plus a verb)*

- *If I were you I would have (add verb)*
- *It looks like (plus a noun)*
- *It's time to (plus a verb)*
- *What if (plus a subject and verb)*
- *How was (plus a noun)*
- *Let's say that (plus subject and verb)*
- *I think I should (plus a verb)*
- *I'm sorry to (plus a verb)*
- *I was thinking about (plus a verb)*
- *I think I should (plus a verb)*
- *Thank you for (plus a verb)*
- *I don't know what to do about (plus a noun)*
- *Have you ever thought about (plus a verb)?*

Using just one of those phrases, you're about to see how many different situations it's suited for:

Have you ever thought about (plus a verb)?

- Have you ever thought about starting your business?
- Have you ever thought about changing jobs?
- Have you ever thought about learning how to swim?
- Have you ever thought about becoming a writer?
- Have you ever thought about having more children?
- Have you ever thought about selling your house?
- Have you ever thought about visiting South America?
- Have you ever thought about learning Russian?
- Have you ever thought about the meaning of life?
- Have you ever thought about joining a fitness center?

If you learned just this one phrase, you can immediately see how many ways you can use it in daily conversation. This phrase, in particular, is a great example because when you ask it, you're inviting someone into a conversation with you.

That will spawn the use of even more sentences using phrases you've already learned.

Can you see how pointless it becomes to learn individual words when your ultimate aim is to speak more fluently? That's not to say that learning more words isn't important. But don't forget to give a priority to learning phrases as well.

3. Think in English

When you go to speak to someone, don't think in your native language and then translate your sentence into English. Simply think in English. This is one of those guidelines that is easier said than done. You're trying to break a habit – thinking in your native tongue – that has been with you all of your life. To be honest, you probably don't know any other way to think.

Why is thinking in your native language, not a particularly good idea? The ordering of the words in your native language is more than language not going to be the same as in the English language. Your natural tendency will be to repeat the English words in that order.

But more than that, in the process of translating your sentence, you'll probably be trying to use grammar rules you're not all that familiar with yet.

Thinking in English will undoubtedly be difficult at first, but the more you force your mind to do it, easier it becomes. And the easier it becomes, the more fluent you'll be in the English language. Give it a try the next time you go to speak English.

4. Practice speaking English when you hear it.

Remember that reading and listening to the English word doesn't make you a better speaker. It will give you more knowledge of reading the written word and understanding it when it is spoken to you. But learning to speak it yourself, requires you do more work. It requires that you truly become interactive with the language.

Without a doubt, reading and listening to the language are two of the most important aspects of learning English. But you're missing the final piece of the puzzle if you don't practice speaking it. This goes for any language, not just English.

Think about the order in which young children learn their native language. They first learn how to speak it and become quite fluent in it and finally learn how to read. Yes, I know that in the process they make many grammatical mistakes. One of the most common is to use the word "brung" as a past tense form of "bring." The correct form is brought. "Look what I've brung you." But the vital point is they didn't wait until they knew what the proper form of the verb was before they spoke. And they do indeed get their message across.

So, don't obsess with reading and listening. It appears the natural order of learning a language is listening, speaking, reading and then writing. So don't think for a moment that your reading and writing skills aren't good enough to allow you to speak it. Your average four-year-old doesn't seem to worry about it.

5. Surround yourself with others who speak English

I've said it before and I'll say it again: immerse yourself in the English language. Compare the English language to an ocean. As long as you stay on the ship you'll only learn what's at the surface of the ocean. Sure, you'll have a great view of the waves and you know the temperature by dipping your hands in the water occasionally. But you'll never know what lies beneath the surface unless you immerse yourself – submerge yourself – into the body of water.

If you don't the plunge from the boat into the ocean right now, when will you?
Think about this for a moment. Those English students who excel at speaking the language are usually the individuals who attended – or are still attending – an English-speaking school. Why is that? Because they were in a culture that forced them to speak English. If they had their way they might have preferred to speak more in their own language.

But they took all their classroom lessons in English, talked to their professors in English – even talked to their friends in English.

Compare these individuals to those who studied abroad, but returned lamenting they still aren't fluent in the language. Because all the while they were in an English-speaking country they never allowed themselves to take the plunge. For whatever reason, they never took the plunge into fully using what skills they had developed up to that time?

So does that mean you have to travel or go to an English-speaking school in order to speak the language fluently? No, not by a long shot. You can become fluent in the language without ever traveling anywhere! Simply make a pact with your friends who are also learning the language that you're all going to dive into the ocean of English to learn what's beneath the surface.

Promise each other that when gathered you'll only speak English. Don't have that many friends who are English speakers or learning the language? Before you know it you'll find yourself thinking in English when you're around these individuals and speaking in the language won't seem so frightening any longer.

Chapter 4: Mistakes Are the Foundation Of Any Good Speaker

"Would you like me to give you a formula for success? It's quite simple, really.
Double your rate of failure."
—Thomas J. Watson, founder of IBM

Right about now, you may be thinking that this chapter is a thinly veiled attempt to make you believe that mistakes are good. They're our "friends" in fact. You may also be thinking that I'm crazy.

But it's true. Mistakes are your "friends." I hate to tell you but the sooner you recognize this, the faster you'll learn the English language.

If you've ever heard any motivational speaker, then you've probably heard that you can only learn if you're willing to make mistakes. This statement is true regardless of what you're doing learning a language to building a multimillion-dollar business.

The speaker, of course, didn't mean that you should purposely set out to make mistakes. What he meant was when you find you've made a mistake, learn from it and continue on.

It's the greatest advice you can be given, in fact, with regard to learning how to speak English. You can only be a fluent speaker if you actually speak it. When you do speak it you're very likely to make mistakes, it's only natural.

In a way, you could say if you're not making any mistakes then you're really not learning much. You may think that's a harsh statement, but it happens to be the truth.

When you hit that plateau of speaking English, then it's vital to break through to the next level as quickly as possible. And the only way to do that is to expose yourself to the possibility of making mistakes in your speech.

For most of us, that means to step outside of your comfort zone. That's a scary proposition for most of us. But you know you have to do it. The following are a few tips on how to practice speaking more despite your fears.

1. Enter a low-risk situation

What's a low-risk situation? It's one that's friendly enough that when you do make mistakes, those around understand and gently correct you. It's a situation in which you trust those with whom you're speaking to understand you're learning.

One of the best situations to put yourself into is to work with other students. You need to ask everyone in the conversation to correct you – diplomatically, of course – when you misspeak or your grammar is horribly incorrect. You, in turn, are confronting your fear and leaving your comfort zone in a limited, controlled way.

So what produces this fear anyway? It seems counter-intuitive that you would fear to speak the very language you've been so enthusiastic about learning. But that's human nature.

You're not alone in your fear. And if you understand the origin of your fear, then you'll be able to grapple with it better. Many psychologists will tell you that the fear of doing something, even learning a language, stems from your thinking that you must speak it perfectly. That is without any mistakes.

You need to ask yourself why you feel this way. What would happen if you did make a mistake in your conversation? The worst-case scenario would be being laughed at, let's say. Your mistake may unintentionally offend someone. Or it may mean that someone misunderstood what you said.

There may be other reasons though you fear mistakes when speaking to others. Perhaps you have the long-held belief that making a mistake is a sign of weakness.

The problem with this line of thinking, though, is that you have molded these thoughts to such gigantic proportions and distorted them so they're all you can see. Now, you've created the mindset that you can't afford the "luxury" of making a mistake in your conversations.

Does this scenario apply to you? If the perfectionist line of thinking is hindering your learning you *can* change your thinking with three easy steps and start speaking English again.

1. First, you need to identify this type of thinking.

This means you must give some thought to why you're hesitating about speaking English in public. Have you been laughed at in the past for mistakes you've made? Perhaps, in making a mistake you've inadvertently offended someone. Now, you're afraid of offending any more individuals.

If you can identify why you're fearful of speaking in public, then you can start to design a strategy to conquer it.

2. List other ways of thinking about this

Once you know the catalyst of your fears, then create a list of other ways of thinking about your speaking English with others. This could include such thoughts as, "Others understand that I'm still learning and will forgive my mistakes," "The more I speak the better I'll become and the fewer mistakes I'll make," "I need to accept these mistakes myself and not only forgive myself for them but learn from them as well."

3. Now review this list of alternative thoughts. Compare it to your perfectionist thinking.

Once you analyze both ways of thinking see if you can't develop another perspective on the situation that will be helpful to your learning and give you a more realistic view of the situation.

It may take some time to change your thinking, but you can if you follow these suggestions. You may even begin speaking a limited amount while you're reviewing your situation.

I have a friend who's still learning English. He speaks it fairly well, but the one situation he hates to find himself in is ordering pizza over the phone. He's terrified he'll order the wrong toppings and he then has a worthless pizza.

So this is how he used these steps to reduce his fears about it. After he calmed down a bit from the thought, he identified his perfectionist thinking: "The person taking my order will think I'm stupid."

He then created alternative thoughts to counter that: "I'm anything but stupid." "I'm using a new language that's not my native tongue." "I'm speaking English the best I can at this point." "Speaking on the phone is a wonderful way to use my English skills." "In fact, the more I take risks like this, the more natural my speaking skills will be," "The more I speak the language, the better I'll be and the more confident I'll be."

Then he evaluated the situation in a new light: "I may be afraid of looking stupid. But I know differently. I'm learning a new language and I'm giving it my best shot. I'm allowed to make mistakes. It is, after all, the only way I'll improve."

And improve you will. The more often you step out of your comfort zone and push yourself to speak English, you'll discover that your English is getting better and better. Why not try it yourself? What have you got to lose – except your fear, that is?

Are You Ready to Accelerate the Learning Process?

Yes, I am talking about mistakes. Just like the individual above you finally took the risk of ordering pizza in English, it's time you take that giant leap to not only accepting your mistakes but embracing them. You've probably heard the story about Thomas Edison, probably the most prolific inventor of the twentieth century. He was asked once how he felt during his failed attempts at finding the proper material for the filament of the light bulb. The individual specifically pointed out that Edison went through nearly 10,000 various materials before he discovered the proper one.

Edison quickly corrected him with this unique perspective on the situation: "I did not fail 9,999 times. I found 9,999 ways of how not to create a light bulb."

As long as you view your mistakes as signs for not learning or reasons why you'll never learn to speak the language, you'll never go beyond the level of fluency you're at right now.

The moment, however, you accept mistakes as not only a natural part of life, but a very necessary tool in the learning process, you'll unleash that hidden power of learning that lies within you.

Now is the time to accept the power of mistakes and press on and expose yourself as often as possible to the English language. Do this not fearful of making mistakes, but vowing to embrace the mistakes and learning from them. This, more than any other piece of advice, will radically change your view of learning the English language.

Here are a few tips to start you off:

1. Find a trusted partner to work with

You can spend all the time you want reading English, but the moment you do you've expanded your world of learning. Grab a partner that's ideally at your level of fluency or better. The idea is to create an atmosphere for learning that embraces – even encourages – mistakes. If you're both at about the same level of development, then you'll discover that you'll benefit from this partnership.

When you're searching for your partner, don't fear from asking someone you know from the internet or a friend in another part of the country. You can always practice the language through the technology of Skype.

You may also want to spend some time exploring the website sharedtalk.org. Here, you'll discover not only students of the English language but native speakers as well. In addition to chat rooms, the site contains "voice rooms," where several individuals can go to comfortably practice the language.

There's just one word of caution in this method. That's the fact that you must find a person who embraces the possibility of mistakes as you do. You both need to know you have that freedom.

2. Refine and expand your learning

Once you've found your partner then it's time to get down to business. You may believe that sitting and talking is an excellent exercise. But think a moment about taking the extra step. Expand and refine your learning by through several strategies.

One of them is to purposely ask your partner to pronounce a few of the vocabulary words you've been using. Then repeat the words after him or her. This works extremely well if your language partner is a native speaker. He'll know the nuances of the spoken word that someone who speaks English as a second language may not.

Another trick to getting the most out of these sessions is to record them, with the permission of your language buddy of course. Then you make reviewing this recording a priority of your next study session when you're alone.

This will take certainly enhance your learning capacity. Even though you believe you'll never forget both the mistakes you made as well as the proper way to speak the words, don't count on it. Your ability to retain all of this information in this situation is limited – and no, not because you're not bright enough.

Rather, in this type of situation, your mind is reassessing and processing so many different things, that not everything you learned in this session may get transferred along to that not everything you learned in this session may get transferred along to our long-term memory. Once you play this information back on a recorder, you'll undoubtedly encounter something you had completely forgotten about.

3. Talk about interesting subjects

What's worse than being engaged in a boring conversation? Being engaged in a boring conversation in which you're still learning the language.

I guarantee you that if you don't choose topics that fully engage you, two things will occur. First, you'll become incredibly bored with the conversation. Second, you'll cut the session short as soon as you get the chance.

But by choosing a topic that you're already interested in – ideally passionate about – you'll discover that you can talk on forever. Not only that but you'll be far less fearful of making mistakes. You'll also be eager to expand your vocabulary and pronunciation of new words.

Fluency in any language is only possible if you learn the subtle art of listening. Don't expect to gain much knowledge if when you do get a chance to speak in English you're too nervous to listen or to busy translating what the others are saying to concentrate on the meaning of the words and the course of the conversation. We discuss this in more depth in the following chapter.

Chapter 5: Improve Your Listening, Your Fluency Will Follow

It's nearly impossible to talk about enhancing your fluency in English without talking about the act of listening. The two are intertwined. The only way to truly speak the language like a native is to listen to those who already speak it well.

While you may believe you've been "listening" all this time, perhaps it's time to dig into what's involved in the listening process – especially the more advanced listening skills that every language student needs. It's actually not extremely difficult to develop these skills. If you simply keep your mind on the conversation at hand, then you're already far along in improving your active listening skills.

There are many reasons to develop such skills, even beyond that of learning a language. Listening is actually a fundamental method of learning knowledge of any type. Think about it, when you were in school you needed to learn how to listen to your instructor or your professor. If you didn't actively listen, you may have found yourself struggling in class.

Active listening in a classroom setting means not only understanding what your teacher is saying but even taking notes on the topic, in order to take a test at a later date.

Once you progress into the business world, you'll discover the ability to listen actively will help you understand customers, clients and colleagues alike.

It should come as no surprise then that active listening is an important aspect of learning how to speak the language. It's how you'll learn what syllables to emphasize in certain words, how to structure sentences and how to make plural nouns out of single nouns. And that's just for starters.

As you go along, you'll soon be recognizing idioms and colloquialisms. And before you know it, you'll be not only understanding them but using them yourself.

Tips for Enhancing your Active Listening Skills

1. Face the speaker, make eye contact and watch him speak

This is excellent advice for anyone engaged in a conversation. It's especially important for those involved in the business. In fact, you may already have developed this habit if you've conducted any type of business in your native language. But this advice is critical to an individual learning the language.

What do you gain by listening this way? Watching him speak will help you see how he forms words with his mouth so you can do the same when you use those words.

2. Pay attention to what the person is saying, but stay relaxed.

Perhaps this is the hardest advice of all when it comes to attentive listening and learning the English language. After all, you're going to be nervous, just making sure you understand what he's saying. It's difficult to stay relaxed, but if you can do just that, you'll actually increase your power of learning.

3. Mentally screen out all distractions

Background noises and movements of those around you are considered distractions. Once you begin to focus on what the English-speaking individual is saying, you'll probably find this comes naturally to you.

If you do find your mind wandering, simply bring it back to the present moment and the speaker. Don't waste any time or energy belittling yourself for your slip up.

4. Listen to the words being said and visualize what the speaker is saying

This is an effective way of immersing yourself in the language. It allows your mind to create related words and images and will help you with your ability to actually think in English. Not only that, but you'll also discover that when you do that, you'll retain the information longer.

After all, what good is learning the language if you don't retain what you're learning?

5. Summarize what the other person has said

In many ways, this is the ultimate test of how well you understand the spoken word. But more than that, by paraphrasing and summarizing what you believe you've just heard, you're actually using all your skills in speaking. Speaking on your feet challenges you to think in English, something you need to learn in order to speak the language better.

Beyond Active Listening

But if that's as far as you've taken your listening skills, then you're actually cheating yourself. You're holding yourself back from quicker, easier fluency in the English language. That's because there's a skill beyond active listening and it's called extensive listening. If you've never heard it, then it's time you not only learn what it is but how to use it to your advantage.

Extensive listening is an amazing tool you can use in practicing your skills at listening to others speak the English language. Basically, it involves taking a topic and listening to it presented in a myriad of different forms – recordings, videos, and interviews, both live and recorded.he

If you had to make one change or add one thing to your learning program, including extensive listening would be the item. It's easy enough to start.

Choose a topic that interests you. If you read the last chapter and have a favorite subject matter you're already talking with your language partner with, it could be that. The alternative is to select a different topic. Consider though how you can expand your language skills if you used the same topic for each exercise.

Whatever topic it is, two things will help you excel at this challenge. The first is to make sure that it's a subject you'll be able to find a good deal of material on. Second, try to make it a topic you already have at least a passing knowledge on. This will definitely facilitate your learning.

Once you've chosen your topic, then begin to research it. You'll be searching for resources that require you to listen. That means reading articles at this point, at least, is not a priority. Think YouTube videos, podcasts, television documentaries and even radio talk shows.

When you listen, especially at first, listen to comprehend the main ideas. At this point, don't worry about many of the details. If you can understand and repeat the important points of the topic, you're doing great.

Choose sources, by the way, that emphasize the basic information. If you delve too far into the topic, you may discover that you become frustrated, especially if it involves the learning of a specialized vocabulary. Of course, the more advanced you are when you start this exercise the more you can dig into the topic.

You may find yourself discarding one topic and choosing another. The initial subject may be beyond your language skills at the moment, or you may find the subject matter to easy depending on where you are in your learning.

Keep in mind during this challenge, that extensive listening is probably the most difficult thing for a language student to do so be prepared to dedicate yourself to this technique.

Not sure what topic to select for this exercise? Below are several general selections. You can begin exploring these to see if anything interests you. In the process, though, it's very likely you'll discover even more interesting topics you'd like to pursue:

1. News stories and biographical information on political leaders and international sports stars.

2. Reviews given in English movies or television programs you've watched in your language.

Thanks to the internet and the myriad of cable networks that the average person is exposed to today, this is an easy topic to research. From here, you may discover an interest in one of the actors or actresses and expand your horizons.

If you're not quite sure where to look for listening material, try a few of these more popular websites:

- Spotlight English
- Ello
- Voice of America

Regardless of the listening technique, you use in your English conversations, the point is to be involved in the present moment. It's difficult to advance your ability to speak English when you're thinking of your grocery list while the other person is speaking. Of course, this is excellent advice for everyone in a conversation whether he's learning the language or speaking his native tongue.

If you've been doing this and still frustrated in what you perceive as a lack of progress, then you'll be interested in learning the incredible breakthrough technique in the following chapter. It's called shadowing and in a moment you'll learn why.

Chapter 6: Shadowing

Pedro sat down for a cup of coffee with a friend. "I've hit a major snag in my ability to speak English," he said. "I've hit this brick wall and can't seem to break through it. I'm not quite sure what to do."

The English student made sure he was talking to his friend in English. He also was attentive when his friend answered in English. "I know you're doing everything right," his friend replied. "You're being an active listener right now."

"So what's my problem?" Pedro asked.

"Perhaps you should try a technique called shadowing," his friend suggested. "Have you ever heard of it?"

Pedro shook his head no.

If like Pedro, you don't know about the technique of shadowing, you may be missing that piece of the language puzzle that will pull your entire learning experience together and have you speaking English like a native in no time.

Shadowing is at least what this method is referred to in academic circles. Many others know it as "parroting." This learning method was originally developed in Germany and then later in Korea. It involves the awesome power of listening with the indispensable power of actually speaking the language.

It's an easy method to implement. You simply listen to a person who has a basic grasp of the language and you repeat – to the best of your ability – what he's saying. You do this immediately after the other individual (or recording) has spoken and you do this whether you understood all of his sentences or not.

According to Dr. Alexander Arguelles, the developer of this method, it's best to be repeating the words while you're walking. In doing so, he said you'll not only enhance your alertness but increase the oxygenation process of your body.

In fact, anyone; who has ever practiced this will testify that there is something – they aren't   quite sure what – about the walking (preferably outdoors) while you repeat what you hear. In fact, many individuals who have successfully performed this method describe it as the closest thing to listening to music and singing along.

No doubt you've done this. Every time you hear your favorite song, you can't help yourself, you end up singing along. If you pay close attention to what is occurring, you'll notice you're singing the words nearly at the same time as the musicians.

If you give this some thought it appears weird, especially because you probably couldn't recall the words unless you hear the start of the song. Then all the words come flooding into your memory without much effort. It's the same mechanism working when you shadow.

The peculiar aspect of learning a song is that you can go decades without hearing it or even thinking about it. The moment you hear even a portion of the tune, you're singing along with it like you heard it yesterday. All the lyrics come flooding back to your memory.

There are actually courses available to get you started. But as you decide whether you want to use them, you may want to try this on your own. This technique isn't that difficult with all the amazing technology that abounds. You can listen to almost anything on your cell phone, take a walk outside and parrot the words almost at the same time the recording is. You can do this with any material from recordings of speakers to audio books.

It's easy enough to get started. Decide on the English audio you'd like to use. If at all possible, choose selections that have an accompanying transcript or at the very least subtitles. The nature of the material doesn't matter. If you have a favorite movie, by all means, choose that. You really couldn't get bored when you're watching and listening to something you enjoy.

Perhaps you have a favorite television show – either a crime drama or a situation comedy. Some individuals recommend such sites as Power English Lessons. You may want to give that site a try.

Prior to actually shadowing this material, you'll be wise to listen to it once without shadowing it to get acquainted with the content. This is especially true if you've never heard it before. It's actually a bit easier to shadow if you have at least a passing familiarity with the piece.

The Process of Shadowing

Once you've initially reviewed the material, start listening to it again. This time your goal is to imitate or parrot the actors and narrator as precisely as possible. The ultimate goal is to repeat everything they're saying.

Ideally, you'll want to say everything they're saying at precisely the same time as the recording. If at first, you're not that familiar with the content, you can wait until the sentence is complete before repeating it.

When parroting the words don't just say them without any feeling. Imitate everything the native speaker is saying, down to the precise pronunciation, the inflection in the voices. If you try to be perfect in all of this, you'll drive yourself stir crazy.

Your goal is to try to keep up. The more often you shadow this material, the better you'll get. So instead of trying to perfect your presentation right from the start, just make up your mind you're going to have fun with this.

Below is an alternative to this specific approach to shadowing which may be more suited to your needs.

1. Start with finding a text at your spoken proficiency level in English.

2. Listen to this once in order to gain a general understanding of it.

This is a great step that many students try to skip only to find they need to stop and perform this ritual from the start – and this time listening to it before you shadow it. First, you'll know for certain if the chosen text really does match your proficiency level.

Secondly, you'll discover if the topic holds your interest. There's nothing worse than try to read something in a language that's not your native language and find it's . . . well, boring. If either of these is the case – too difficult or too boring – then go back and select another text.

3. Listen to the piece a couple of more times.

When you do this, you'll be sure to be confident in your ability to know what the text is talking about. You don't have to fully understand everything *before* you shadow it, but at least you know you'll eventually be able to figure it out.

4. If there are any words you don't know the meaning of looking them up before going any farther.

That's right! Before you start shadowing look up the words you aren't positive you know. It may take a little more time, upfront before you shadow, but I promise you it'll save you time later in the exercise.

5. Listen to the text at least once a day.

Listen more than this if it's at all possible.

6. Pronounce the same piece until you can repeat it at the same speed as the recording.

7. Move on to another piece in the English language.

Approach the second piece in the same manner as you did the first.

Why Walking and Talking?

While you're shadowing remember that the ultimate way for this to work is by walking – preferably outside – while you're repeating the language. Don't overlook this seemingly inconspicuous aspect of this exercise. Why is this so important? According to some, and you probably have experienced this yourself, it's actually quite difficult to have your brain focus on learning a language while your body is trying to walk.

Think back to when you were learning how to drive. If you were like most of us, the first several times you were behind the wheel of a car you didn't talk much. You probably turned the radio or CD player down or even off as well. Once you conquered the act of driving, though, you felt much more comfortable listening to music or talking to your passengers.

There's a very good reason for this. It's difficult for the human mind to speak a language you're unfamiliar with and perform another activity. While at first, you'll find this next to impossible (but don't give up on it) as you continue, you'll see improvement.

Shadowing while you're walking is challenging your brain. It's forcing your mind to understand new language skills and eventually train your body to accept speaking this language as an automated process. That, in the end, is exactly what you want: to speak English without giving it a second thought.

The Scriptorium Method

At about the same time Dr. Arguelles developed shadowing, he also created a related method for learning the spoken word. This technique, by contrast, combines the power of repeating words out loud with of the reinforcement of writing them on paper. It's called the *scriptorium method* and you may already be unwittingly using it. It might even be a method you've used in your native language as a youngster learning spelling words.

Instead of just working with words, you'll be working with sentences at least initially. Create a sentence or choose the one you've already learned. Get a piece of lined notebook paper and begin writing the sentence. Instead of writing it all at once, however, write it deliberately. As you copy each word, pause momentarily and say the word out loud. Then – and only then – can you continue to the next word.

If, for example, you were using the first line of Charles Dickens' **A Tale of Two Cities,** you would use this sentence: "It was the best of times; it was the worst of times." Now grab your pen and paper and begin. Write the word it, pause and then say it. Do the same for "was." Write it down and pronounce it. Write and speak each word in the sentence until you've completed each word.

No, you aren't quite done – not yet at least. Now that you've written it on the page say the entire sentence out loud. Pause for a moment. Do this again with the same sentence a minimum of ten to fifteen times. That purpose of this exercise isn't simply to recognize the words when you see them, but to actively speak them.

If you want you can now move on to another sentence. Some individuals choose to work from the sentences of a novel like this (although *A Tale of Two Cities* would take quite a while). Another option would be to copy and recite sentences from any of your lessons.

This is a great secondary method of learning pronunciation, especially if the option of shadowing is unavailable to you. The aim of writing and pronouncing words, like in shadowing, uses more than one sensory organ of your body. By combining these organs, you'll be increasing the chances that you'll remember not only the structure of the sentences but the pronunciation of the words.

Use this interactive approach to the English language as often as you can fit it into your allotted time to study. You'll be amazed at how much faster you'll learn how to speak the language simply by writing and pronouncing your words and phrases once a week.

In the next chapter, you'll learn one simple habit that just about all successful English students have used at one time in order to improve the ability to speak English and sound like a native.

Chapter 7: Secrets of a Fluent English Speaker

If you've been struggling with soaring to the next level of the spoken English language, then you may have already been asking yourself this one question, "What are those students who are excelling in this area doing that I'm not?"

And you're right to ask that question. That's the only way you can diagnose what you're doing compared to what they're doing. Here's a surprise. Usually, it comes down to one exercise. One simple ten-minute exercise to be exact. This habit helps to thoroughly immerse these individuals in the language.

This chapter explains how you can use this incredibly powerful tool to aid you in soaring to the next level of fluency in speaking English.

Read a Book (Yes, in English!) out loud

What if you knew that there was one simple exercise that could totally transform the way you spoke the English language? That if you participated in this routine every day for as little as ten minutes, you'd be building your English speaking ability, not unlike an athlete improves his skill through daily practice?

Imagine what it would be like to speak the English language like a native without even the need to venture into any conversation with another person? If this sounds too good to be true, think again. You're about to be introduced to a simple ten-minute daily method that will do just that.

Not only that but this simple method can help you keep up with those conversations among native speakers who ordinarily speak so fast that most students get lost and even discouraged.

Simply reading a book written in English out loud. Yes, that's all there is to it. But there are a few criteria that go along with this exercise. The first caveat is that you have to read the words as fast as you can while retaining proper pronunciation. At first, this may seem like you're reading at a snail's pace, but as you continue to practice you'll find yourself getting faster and comprehending the words more quickly.

Part of the key to this is the careful and deliberate pronunciation of words. Keep in mind that pronunciation depends on you to open and move your mouth properly. When you pay attention to the movement of your mouth, you'll be pleasantly surprised at the improvement in your pronunciation.

Many individuals try this suggestion but are, quite frankly, just a bit skeptical of it. They're not quite sure how reading a book out loud – to no one in particular, in fact, could increase their skill. So why does it work?

1. This exercise is doing nothing less than creating an oral atmosphere around you.

If you're anything like the average student learning English as a second language, English is probably seldom if ever spoken in your home. This exercise, then, is an awesome way to practice speaking the language when you aren't in touch with others who speak it, even on a rudimentary level.

Try to invest at least ten minutes daily reading out loud five days a week. In fact, why not try it for a month. At the end of the month, see if you notice any changes in your fluency.

2. Reading out loud increases your opportunity for retention.

Not only does it increases your chances to retain more of what you read, you increase this opportunity by approximately 100 percent when compared to reading silently. When you read silently you use two parts of your body – your brain and your eyes. While this is good, reading out loud actually doubles the number of body parts involved in the process. This activity forces you to not only use your brain and your eyes but your ears and voice as well.

Scientists have discovered that this really does double your retention of the material. You're not only thinking about the language and seeing it, but you're also hearing it and saying it.

There is possibly no better way to actually immerse yourself in the English language. While you're reading you're actually subconsciously soaking up the thinking and speech patterns of the language. But that's not all, you're also enhancing your ability to remember in English as well as communicate in the language.

3. You're exercising your facial muscles.

Yes, this isn't the most exciting result of this habit, but it is more important than you think. The sounds involved in speaking the English language are formed through the passing of the air through a certain segment of our facial organs.

As you probably already know through your studies, the sounds are then formed through the use of your lips, nose, teeth, tongue and other facial features. When you're learning a new language, there are many new sounds you need to learn in order to speak it properly. At first, it may seem that you're totally incapable of pronouncing certain sounds.

Many individuals whose first language is Spanish have a difficulty enunciating the letter "z" in English. Spanish doesn't contain that sound. But just for your information, native English speakers sometimes have a hard time with the "rr" sound of Spanish. This is not a natural sound for them to use. In each case, the individual needs to develop the specific muscles for proper pronunciation.

4. You'll learn how to become responsible for correcting yourself.

You've been studying the English language that you're already fairly proficient in the proper enunciation of it. Don't be surprised that as you read out loud, you'll slowly begin to "police yourself."

Eventually, you'll hear yourself pronounce one or more of the words incorrectly. When you first start this habit, you may slide by this. After you're established in this habit, though, you'll discover yourself, stopping and pronouncing it again properly. That's exactly one of the goals of this exercise.

5. Reading out loud increases your oral fluency.

There's no way around it, reading a book or newspaper out loud must improve your fluency in English. Ideally, you'll want to take time out of your morning to read out loud. And yes, I do mention this for a reason. This short, simple exercise loosens your speech organs, getting them accustomed to making the sounds of English.

Not only that, doing it before class jogs your memory of the sounds necessary for the language. You'll soon discover that your fluency will be greatly enhanced on those days you take the time to do this exercise.

One of the great things about this exercise, you can choose a book that actually interests you. Choose a novel you've always wanted to read or one of your favorite authors. If you're a sports fan, for example, then you could read an autobiography of your favorite athlete or merely read the sports section of the newspaper daily.

Remember, though, that you'll gain the most from this exercise when you read actively or observantly. What do I mean by that? Be totally involved in what you're reading. Use your mind taking note of not only the material being presented but the structure of the sentences as well the order of the words in sentences. Ideally, you'll transfer these observations into your daily practices. And the next thing you know you're speaking English like you were born into it.

Chapter 8: Idioms and More: You Can't be Fluent without Idioms

Hmm? Did you notice that title of this chapter? Yes, part of it is what's known as an idiom. In fact, that's probably one of the most common idioms native speakers use.

The English language can be a struggle to learn on its own. Throw in an unexpected idiom or two and now you've opened a whole new can of worms. There again, is another idiom. Just for your information, opening a whole new can of worms means that in an attempt to solve one problem an entirely different problem popped up.

Even children who are native to the language have a difficult time learning some of the idioms if they've never heard them before. When I was a child, for example, and an older one at that, my mom and I were finishing up washing the dishes after supper one day. My father, who had gone into the living to read a book, actually fell asleep reading it. The book lay on his chest.

Mom said to me. I need to "take a page from Dad's book." I was horrified. "But, Mom," I said, "that would confuse him to no end." My mother looked at me like I was crazy. She was using an idiom and I was taking her words literally. I thought she was going to pull a prank on my father by actually confusing him by tearing a physical page from the book he was currently reading. As an avid reader, I didn't even say where the humor was in the act. What she meant, though, was that she was going to follow his example and take a nap.

Knowing the confusion I had with several idioms, who knew as I got older that I actually confused my own child with one. I said to her, in all innocence one time, that something I did would undoubtedly get her Dad's goat. She said to me (as if I weren't already aware of it), "But Mom, Dad doesn't have a goat."

Now as you probably have already guessed getting someone's goat has nothing to do with stealing his farm livestock. What I meant by that was I was going to agitate him, get him worried and perhaps even a little concerned about something. But my daughter, like myself before her, had to learn the language one idiom at a time.

How to Learn Idioms

Right now you're probably thinking that an idiom is a secret joke that native speakers like to pull on non-native speakers and children. Who knows? Perhaps that's exactly how idioms did come into use hundreds of years ago. Now there they are common phrases that are widely accepted in the English.

Unfortunately for the serious student of English, there is really no way to learn them except by memorizing them one by one. While there are really probably hundreds of them, I'm providing you with the meanings of the ten most commonly used idioms in the English language.

These are the ones you're most likely to encounter as you begin to delve deeper into the language. If you can begin by learning these ten, you'll probably reduce your confusion of listening to native speakers by quite a bit. You'll then be able to focus more on the other parts of the conversations you're listening to.

10 of the Most Common Idioms

1. **A piece of cake**

You'll hear this quite a bit. "That test was a piece of cake," someone might say walking out of a classroom. That means that it presented no challenge to them. It represented, in fact, quite the opposite -- something easy to accomplish. Another, related idiom, meaning much the same thing is "easy as pie." Why anyone would compare a pie to something being easy isn't really understood, but at least you now know the meaning of both of these.

2. **It cost an arm and a leg**

That would be a gory financial transaction if you were to take this phrase literally. This idiom means the item being referred to was expensive. It's used nearly constantly in this language. In fact, you've probably already heard it.

The Second idiom with a very similar meaning is "it broke the bank." It doesn't mean that the bank – whatever or wherever that might be – literally broke into pieces or that it ran out of money. The phrase just means the cost of the item was quite expensive. In both of these cases, many times the implication is that the cost is more than what the item is worth.

3. Break a leg

Believe it or not, this idiom means "good luck." It's especially used backstage in theaters just prior to actors going on stage. It's considered bad luck to say the phrase "good luck" backstage, but apparently, it's all right to wish someone to break a bone. It's widely used outside of this venue as well. So the next time someone tells you to "break a leg" they really aren't hoping you trip and fall.

4. Let the cat out of the bag

Here's another curious phrase. After all, who would place a perfectly good cat in the bag in the first place? And who would care if the cat got out? This phrase's true meaning, though, is to reveal something that was meant to be kept a secret. When someone tells you something and you inadvertently tell another, you're "letting the cat out of the bag."

5. Hit the books

Idioms can certainly conjure up some bizarre images in the minds of those who aren't native speakers. Upon first hearing this, perhaps you had an image of students surrounding themselves with the textbooks they like least and physically punching and hitting them. What a strange way of releasing your anger. This phrase is really synonymous with the act of studying. Yes, it's that simple. Not nearly as colorful, though.

6. Hit the nail on the head

When you hear this one you may believe you're speaking to a carpenter. But that's not necessarily so. In fact, chances are good the person who uttered this expression has never even used a hammer in his life. Once again, like with all good idioms, it hasn't a single thing to do with the physical item it's referring to.

Instead, it has everything to do with performing a right move, action, or even the proper interpretation of a fact or statistic. At least with this idiom, it's nearly understandable how it might have got its start. When you take a hammer and hit the nail on the head, the nail glides perfectly into the wood. With the idiom, you've done everything right.

7. To scratch, someone else's back.

You may also hear this phrase as "You scratch my back and I'll scratch yours." This doesn't mean that you'll be literally standing behind someone asking them exactly where there back itches and then he'll do the same for you. Although implied in this literal interpretation is that both individuals are helping the other.

This often-used idiom means that if you help your friend with a problem or out of a tight situation, he'll return the favor when you need something done.

8. When pigs fly

Can you imagine anything more ridiculous than looking up in the sky and seeing a pig fly? They definitely weren't designed with flight in mind – regardless of how they may in evolve in the future.

So just the idea of pigs flying is utterly ridiculous. And there you have it. That's the entire point of this idiom. When pigs fly refers to an event that is highly unlikely if ever, to occur.

9. Bite off more than you can chew

Do you recognize this idiom from the title of this chapter? While this has nothing to do with eating, with a little thought, you might be able to figure it out. Imagine you're starved and have been waiting in a restaurant for a meal that's more than a little late. By the time you get your sandwich you grab it and take a huge bite. Unfortunately, it's a bit more than your mouth can handle and you find it extremely difficult to deal with this situation in a polite and mannered fashion.

While this has absolutely nothing to do with food, it has everything to do with your trying to attempt a feat that is just a bit beyond your capabilities. If you've ever volunteered to perform a project for work only to discover you don't have the knowledge or skill to complete it, then you've bitten off more than you can chew. You've taken on a project that is just too large or beyond your capability to handle at the moment.

Homophones, Homonyms, and Homographs

Just when you think the English language can't get any more difficult to understand, someone has to start talking about homophones, homonyms, and homographs. It's bad enough that each of these words sounds and looks so similar, just wait until you discover what each word represents. Learning about these categories of words alone will convince you if you need any more evidence, that the English language is not the easiest language to learn.

So what are they and why in the world should you even learn them? Let's tackle them one by one. A homophone, also called a homonym, is a word that has at least two distinct, usually unrelated meanings but is pronounced the same in each situation. Sometimes they have the same spelling, but not necessarily.

What do we mean by that? Look at the word rose. "The rose bloomed today." Used in this sentence you know that the word is referring to a flower. But in the sentence, "Diana rose from her nap" means something entirely different, even though they are the same word, spelled the same way.

When you read these words in sentences, you're likely to immediately know the meaning intended. When you and others use them as part of the spoken language you may have to listen closely to know what the word means in the context that it's used.

The use of all types of homophones in the English language is just another good argument for something we talked about earlier in the book: learning to recognize phrases instead of just words.

If you only learned words singly in your early years of language study, you may be puzzled by the use of the word rose in either of those sentences. Depending on what you learned, you may very well be picturing a flower when a person said "rose" instead of the verb, meaning to get up.

As you progress in your study, you'll recognize more and more of these. Here is just a small sampling of homophones:

Lacks – to be without something
Lax – not strict

See – to use your eyes
Sea – a body of water

Erie – one of the Great Lakes in the Midwest of the US
Eerie – a strange feeling, usually referring to something that is paranormal

Vein – blood vessels of mammals
Vain – to attempt something but have it not mean anything

Male – a man
Mail – letters that are delivered by the post office

On to Homographs

If you're not confused enough already, you just may be after you learn about words that are commonly called homographs. These words, more likely a pair of words, are normally spelled identically. The catch is they mean something different depending on their pronunciation. Again, these belong to a class that you'll discover as you continue speaking the English language tests not only your skills but your patience as well.

Sometimes the pair of homographs is pronounced differently. The difference, however, is a subtle one. It's usually just a matter of the placement of the accent in the syllables that make up the word.

One thing you may want to know is that there exists an entire class of homographs that end in the three letters "ate." When they are pronounced one way they have one meaning and when you shift the accented syllable they mean something else.

A classic example of this is the word "advocate." When you pronounce it with the long "a" sound the meaning of the word is to be in support of something. When the word is pronounced with a short "a" sound, the word means a person who either supports or acts on behalf of the cause of another individual.

Unfortunately for the student of the English language, these words are strewn all around. You'll never know where or when you might encounter them. But as you progress in your ability to speak the language you'll discover that you'll become much more familiar with them and recognize them when you both read and listen to the language. Below are just a few of the more common homographs you may encounter in your studies:

- **Attribute:** a characteristic or quality of something or to assign a characteristic to a specific person, place or thing
- **Axes:** the plural of the noun ax or the plural of the noun axis
- **Bass:** a deep tone or a type of fish
- **Bat:** a piece of equipment used to hit a baseball or the winged mammal
- **Compact:** something small or to make something small. It also refers to a case that holds makeup. Additionally, you'll occasionally find this word meaning

agreement or covenant, as in the historic Mayflower Compact.

- **Compound:** something created from more than one substance or an enclosed area that includes at least one building
- **Content:** Satisfied or something that is found in an enclosed case. It also means the words found in books or other material
- **Desert:** an arid, dry place; to leave someone behind. Not to be confused with dessert, which is a sweet after-dinner treat.
- **Does:** a form of the verb do; the plural of doe, a female deer
- **Down:** the opposite of up or soft, young feathers of birds
- **Entrance:** the area in which you enter a room or to bewitch or delight an individual
- **Fine:** sharp or very thin or the penalty you pay
- **Lead**: to take a group behind you and show them the way or a type of metal
- **Minute:** 60 seconds or a portion of an hour
- **Object:** another word for anything you can see or touch or to speak up against something
- **Produce:** fresh fruits and vegetables as in the produce department of a grocery store or to create something
- **Refuse:** a verb meaning to decline something or a noun referring to garbage or waste
- **Row:** a fight or to move a boat with oars
- **Second:** a portion of a minute or the item after the first
- **Tear:** the water that comes from the eyes or to rip
- **Wind:** moving air or to turn in a circular motion
- **Wound:** an injury or something that has been turned, the past tense of wind

While much of this information is important in the written language, it's also fundamental to your acquiring better skills when it comes to the spoken word. If you hear one of these words spoken and need to take time out of your listening trying to decide what it means, you're also losing vital listening time for other portions of the conversation. In fact, in doing that, you may be missing the most important parts of the conversation.

Chapter 9: Contractions in the English Language

One thing you've undoubtedly discovered about the English language is its apparent randomness. As soon as you learn a grammatical rule or a way to pronounce a word you discover at least one exception to the rule. There you are thinking you were making progress. Now you're only left confused.

While it may not make you feel any better but everyone who learns this language has the same problems. We've already mentioned even native speakers have encountered these same problems and some of them have never fully conquered them.

One of the idiosyncrasies of the English language – and one that seems to confuse many students – is the contraction. Students and native speakers alike have problems knowing when to use them and when not to. Some individuals have problems knowing what the contraction even stands for.

If you're having these problems or try to avoid speaking with contractions for fear of making a fool of yourself join the club. But now, we're going to give you a quick course in this unique part of the English language. Before you've completed this chapter you'll be not only using contractions like a native speaker, but you'll know exactly why and how you're using them.

What is a contraction, anyway?

In its basic form, a contraction is a shortened form of a word or two words. It's created, in its most common written form by omitting a letter or letters and replacing them with an apostrophe.

Contractions are normally used in spoken English. Not always found in the written language, a contraction represents syllables that have been dropped by native speakers because on the whole, they speak fast and simply compress the words together. One of the ones you've probably encounter frequently is "can't" for "cannot."

You may already be using this one and a few others. They are, after all, a more informal way to speak and they actually make you sound more like a native speaker. You're less likely to find them in the written language except in some informally written books, like this one whose writing style is to sound more conversational.

Essentially, English uses two types of contractions. The first variety is the type we've just defined, in which one or more letters are missing and replaced by an apostrophe. The list below contains a comprehensive list of contractions you may hear people speak, but it's not necessarily complete.

These contractions have been used for hundreds of years and agreed upon as it were by speakers of the English language. Due to the possibility of being misunderstood, it's widely accepted in the spoken language that individuals don't randomly create their own set of contractions. While these words are definitely the informal presentation of two words they are widely accepted by linguists.

Below are many contractions and the words they represent:

Contraction	Original
aren't	are not
can't	cannot
couldn't	could not
didn't	did not
doesn't	does not
don't	do not
hadn't	had not
hasn't	has not
haven't	have not
he'd	he had, he would
he'll	he will, he shall
he's	he is, he has
I'd	I had, I would
I'll	I will, I shall
I'm	I am
I've	I have
isn't	is not
it's	it is, it has
let's	let us
mustn't	must not
shan't	shall not
she'd	she had, she would
she'll	she will, she shall
she's	she is, she has
shouldn't	should not

that's	that is, that has
there's	there is, there has
they'd	they had, they would
they'll	they will, they shall
they're	they are
they've	they have
we'd	we had, we would
we're	we are
we've	we have
weren't	were not
what'll	what will, what shall
what're	what are
what's	what is, what has
what've	what have
where's	where is, where has
who'd	who had, who would
who'll	who will, who shall
who're	who are
who's	who is, who has
who've	who have
won't	will not
wouldn't	would not
you'd	you had, you would
you'll	you will, you shall
you're	you are
you've	you have
you aren't	you are not

There's technically one other form of contraction, even though few people ever refer to it as such. That's the contractions that

English uses in front of full names to identify gender or occupation. In these, only a few letters of the original word is used and when writing them English rules state you place a period at the end. They should cause you absolutely no problem when you're speaking the language, just be aware of the pronunciation if you read any material aloud in your daily practice.

Mr.	Mister
Mrs.	Mistress
Dr.	Doctor
Atty.	Attorney
Rev.	Reverend

Learning contractions will go a long way in helping you to speak the English language more fluently. In fact, once you feel comfortable and confident using them – as well as understanding others who use them – you'll be well on your way to speaking the language like a native.

Conclusion

At this point of the book, you may be tempted to say that you've finished reading about breaking through to the new level of fluency in the English language. And you're certainly have completed the reading portion of this vital journey. However, you're far from completing your journey.

In one of the most vital ways, you've only just begun. Now that you know what it takes to learn how to reach that breakthrough level of the spoken English language, there will be no stopping you. You're beginning your journey of submerging yourself in English, taking up the challenge of speaking it whenever and wherever you can.

Congratulations. You've made a wise decision to continue to work toward your goals and not allowing anything to hold you back. Armed with the guidelines, suggestions, tips, and techniques in this book and your own personal study and speaking habits that have been successful for you, you'll discover great success.

If your goal is to get a promotion at work, you can rest assured you'll be one of the prime candidates. If your goal is to earn better grades in school, you'll discover the aid in this book will provide you with the foundation you need.

Or perhaps you're learning English simply because your children are beginning to learn it in school. In any case, it's a skill that will be most vital to your future.

There are as many reasons for learning the English language as there are individuals using it. Regardless of your reason for learning it, you'll discover that once you put your mind to it, you'll have no problem.

If, anytime along with your journey, you feel as if you can't take another step or don't know how to go any further, simply open this book again and begin referring to it. Haven't been shadowing like you used to? Perhaps that's why you should be doing once again to breakthrough to yet another level of fluency.

Sometimes we get so involved in the day-to-day activities of life, that we forget to spend the time on goals that mean a lot to us. Sometimes we lose the ardor and excitement we had when we first started the project. If you believe that this is happening to you, why not just review one more time why you wanted to speak English in the first place. Review with yourself why you wanted to speak it as if it were your first language.

Of course, it's natural to feel a bit frustrated by the brick wall you seem to have it if you're feeling as if you're not progressing. Of course, it's natural to feel a bit frustrated by the brick wall you seem to have it if you're feeling as if you're not progressing in your pursuit.

This is the perfect time to refer to your S.M.A.R.T. goals again. When you read over these again, try to capture the excitement you felt when you originally wrote them. Hopefully, the goals were internally stimulated. That means you created them because you felt deeply serious about pursuing them for your own reasons.

If your reasons were because others were telling you that was what you should be doing, then it will be more difficult to recapture that magic that you initially felt. Even if they were externally stimulated, chances are that you felt so confident while learning the language that you adapted these goals as an internal challenge for yourself.

Here are two tips to help you stay with the program, as the English idiom goes:

You've already set your S.M.A.R.T. goals. Initially, it really didn't matter the language. But now use both languages but don't stop there. From these goals, create what many would call a vision board. Remember earlier in the book, we used the goal of being able to give a presentation at work. Write this goal out and then find a photo of a boardroom or an office to represent the presentation and the desire to progress in your career.

If your desire was to keep up with your children's increasing knowledge of the English language which they learning at school, then take a photo of them and put next to that goal. You get the idea. Doing just this will revitalize you.

But then how do you maintain this excitement? Make sure you place these boards in a location in which you can see them, even briefly on a daily basis.

Each time you do see it, repeat your goal out loud. You may even want to stop for a moment and reflect on what this goal means not only to you but to your entire family.

Imagine how proud your children will be of you, for example, when you visit their teachers on the next parent-teacher conference day, speaking like a native speaker. Imagine how your career will soar when you improve your English enough to actually in front of your supervisors and colleagues and talk about the project in English.

Want to Go that Extra Step with Reminders?

Why not take advantage of the current state of technology and set daily or periodic reminders on your phone on what your true goals are in your studies. If you reflect at least once daily at a specific time every day, you'll be keeping these goals in your consciousness. In this way, you'll be less likely to get depressed over your studies and more likely to stay enthusiastic and centered.

 Well Done! Look how far you've come since you took your first step. Remember to have a consistent English practice schedule every day. Keep up the good work. Before you know it, you'll be speaking fluent English like a native.

Accent Reduction For Professionals

How to eliminate your accent to sound more American

Whitney Nelson

Table of Contents

Introduction

It may frustrate you endlessly – especially as a professional with goals of being successful in your career. The fact that many find your accent "charming" doesn't compensate much. It certainly doesn't mean it'll make you successful.

Of course, your accent is less than charming when it prevents someone from understanding what you're saying. It's less than charming when you find yourself repeating yourself. It's especially frustrating and less than charming when you discover that your accent is actually preventing you from advancing in your chosen career.

While this book is useful to all individuals who wish to reduce their accent and sound more like a native speaker, it's written with the professional individual in mind. If your English language skills are solid, your grasp of the vocabulary solid and you're comfortable speaking the language itself, then you may very well be searching for the last piece of the puzzle. Eliminating the accent so you can not only be understood a bit more easily, but feel like you're a better fit into your office environment.

As sad as it may seem, a strong accent when speaking English can actually keep you from achieving your career goals as well as reaching your full potential. It has been proven that when some individuals continually ask you to repeat yourself, it can lower your chances of professional advancement. In other words, enunciating your words and using correct grammar are two requirements to conquer the business world today.

I know how serious you are about your career. Because of this, I also know how serious you are about improving both your pronunciation and in the process reducing and eliminating your accent. This book deals specifically with helping you speak more like a native.

Working with Your Accent

Before you get the wrong idea, there's absolutely nothing "wrong" with a foreign accent. Everyone – even native speakers of English – have some type of accent. Have you ever traveled to Boston or New York and listened in on conversations residents of those cities hold on the street?

Arguably, there are also situations when you can use your accent to your advantage. If you want to move from being considered at "very good" at the English language to the next level, "excellent," then you need to make a concerted effort to help soften your accent.

We'll help you do just that. Once you've conquered your accent, you'll notice how confident you are in talking not only to your supervisors, colleagues, and clients, but also at making presentations.

What is an Accent?

In the largest sense of the word, an accent is how you sound when you speak. Generally speaking, there are two types of accents. The first is what is most commonly identified as a "foreign" accent. This accent is the natural lingering effects of learning, let's say English, using (consciously or unconsciously) the rules or sounds of your native language.

It's actually a coping mechanism if you really think about it. When you're learning English as a second language, you may encounter some difficulty making all of the sounds of English. There are several sounds that no other language contains. Or it could be that your mouth isn't cooperating because it never had to say these sounds before.

The accent occurs when you substitute similar sounds, drawn from your native language. It's called a "foreign" accent simply because it sounds "foreign" to those who are native speakers of English.

The second type of accent, which we lightly touched on earlier, is the one which is used by a specific group of native speakers, usually clustered in a general geographical location. These individuals have cultivated certain pronunciations that are unique to them. Consider the classic Boston accent. Or the accent you'll find among many in New York City. If you travel the United States at all, you'll discover variations of accents. From North Carolina to Kentucky to Texas, each of these areas contains their own accents.

Why are some Sounds Difficult for Some Individuals?

Some people, you'll notice, have a difficult time with sounds that are new to them. The truth is, if you would have learned these sounds when you were an infant, you wouldn't have any trouble at all with them. Children are born with the amazing ability to be able to pronounce all the sounds of every language.

As an infant matures, however, she or he soon learns which specific sounds are important in his language. He then simply ignores the others. If the sounds don't serve the infant and he doesn't use them, you can see how easily it could be for that ability to slip away.

Linguists say that by the time children reach one year of age, they've intuitively learned which sounds don't serve them and simply disregard them. As we age then, these sounds become increasingly more difficult to pronounce.

Individual sounds aren't the only reason you may find yourself speaking with an accent. There are elements of any language called "sound patterns." Specific sound patterns naturally differ among languages. To fully understand this you'll need to look an example or two.

A syllable in an English word may begin or end with a cluster of consonants, like "str" and "ngth." Right now, think of the word strength. This word contains both of those. This is different than the Japanese language, in which a typical syllable contains no more than one consonant immediately followed by one vowel. The examples here are in "ma" or "ki."

For native Japanese speakers, pronouncing these consonant clusters can be problematic. This is why they may place a vowel sound between the consonants in an English cluster.

Another cause of a foreign accent may be derived from the natural sentence structuring of the language. This problem often crops up in Russian. An excellent example is found in the English sentence "The house is very large." The problem for the native speaking Russian is that there is no word corresponding to the English word "the." Therefore, he doesn't see it as essential to speaking it in English.

The second problem is that Russian doesn't require the speaker to place the verb "is" in the sentence. So, if you're translating the sentence into English, the typical Russian speaker would be inclined to simply say, "House very large." While it sounds perfect to the Russian ear, it sounds clumsy to the English ear.

Is Eliminating Accent Really Necessary?

Many students of English ask if eliminating their accent is really necessary. For some, it may not be. There are many individuals who take great pride in their accent. My grandmother, whose first language was Slovak never lost her accent. I suspect that she retained it out of a sense of pride. That doesn't mean she didn't have a great grasp of English.

She did. She lived to be 87 years old and always talked with an accent. But then, she was essential a farmer and a stay-at-home mom.

Examine your career honestly and you'll probably come to the conclusion that it would help you immensely. If you find yourself having difficulty communicating with others due to the way you speak the English language, you may consider reducing it. Just what are the "difficulties" you may experiencing? A very few of these are listed below:

People not understanding you.

I can't tell you how many of my friends and family refuse to go to an excellent doctor or another medical specialist because they have difficulty understanding their strong accent. I can't help but think it's a shame to not avail themselves of what could possibly be the best possible health care they may get.

In many college settings, students give up or refuse to take certain courses because the instructor or professor speaks with a foreign accent. As with the health profession, a student may be passing up the chance to experience a great course.

Avoiding social interaction with those who may not understand you.

In these instances, you're missing out on what may be the best areas of your life, getting together with good friends. Why cut yourself off from social interactions needlessly?

Frustration from having to repeat yourself all the time.

Many individuals find it frustrating to have to continually repeat themselves because they can't be understood. You may not only be frustrated when you speak, you may also hesitate to speak. Why not enjoy all the aspects of a good conversation and the interactions of good friends?

People focusing on your accent more than on what you are trying to say.

We mentioned this problem at the opening of the introduction. There are some individuals who'll find your accent "charming" and get lost in the melodious sounds and ignore the message. If this happens to you, think about reducing your accent. You'll find they're less likely to comment on your accent and more willing to talk about the substance of what you said.

When Problems Turn Into Barriers

But these problems with communication go deeper than what I've outlined above. When the problems are severe enough and occur frequently, these seemingly minor problems can avalanche into barriers in any number of ways. They could hinder your job performance, your advancement in college as well as making your personal life less than satisfying.

So many individuals also tell me their accent is lowering their self-esteem. It's easy to see why. Having to repeat yourself, trying to get your point across and just thinking twice before saying anything in public is sure to have some effect on how you view yourself.

Before you begin to think that it's impossible to eliminate your foreign accent, I'm here to tell you that it's not only possible, but probably easier than what you believe it to be. With even a little concentration and practice you'll find yourself speaking like a native in no time at all.

The key words, though, are concentration and practice. It's not something that's going to happen overnight. Then, again, you probably already know this because you didn't learn how to speak English overnight.

Right now you're so close to mastering the language it would be a shame if you didn't take that extra step to eliminate that accent.

What's In This Book to Help You?

This book is divided into ten chapters, starting explaining why strong accents can reduce your chances of getting hired. It's difficult to have any type of career if you can't get past the first hurdle getting hired.

From there, I take you through the most important steps you'll need to take in order to speak more like a native. Together, we'll be reviewing the various sounds that usually trick and trip those who have learned English as a second language, such as the vowel sounds – a, e, i, and u – as well as what syllables to stress with certain words.

In addition, you'll learn what the soft palate is and why it's important in reducing your accent. This book will provide you with examples and exercises you can use to help in this area.

There are certain letters and sounds in English that can even challenge native speakers. Take the "r" sound for example. Native Japanese speakers naturally find this sound difficult. But you'd be amazed at how many individuals who have learned English as their native language also stumble on this.

I should know. As a grade-school student, I went to speech therapy to learn the proper way to pronounce the letter "r." To this day, I find myself occasionally, not pronouncing it properly, especially if I'm tired.

Sounds like the "th" may be difficult for you to say, which may, in turn, contribute to your accent. There are few, if any, other languages that even have this sound. So, it's naturally a problem for many people who are learning English as a second language.

But that's not all you'll learn in this small book. We'll review intonation, which is nothing more than the natural melody, flow, and pitch of a language, the use of diphthongs (two letters strung together to make one sound) which aren't found in all other languages.

You'll also discover how to put all these disparate segments of the English language together. You'll discover in the last two chapters of this volume, not only how to combine all this learning, but the best methods of practicing them.

It may sound overwhelming at the moment, but as you tackle each of these areas one by one, you'll notice how your accent softens and with time, patience and practice actually disappears.

Are you ready to start your next step in learning the English language – that of reducing and eventually eliminating your accent?

Then, let's get started.

Chapter 1: Is Your Strong Accent Preventing you from Getting your Perfect Job?

It's not fair, you might say. You'd be right. Nonetheless, it occurs every day.

Imagine this scenario. Two individuals interview for the same position with a corporation. Both are equally qualified. One speaks English like a native. The other person speaks with a foreign accent. Who gets the job?

If you said the native speaker, then you already know the odds are swinging that way. Everyone knows that potential employers can't discriminate in the hiring process based on race or gender. But what if an individual were denied a position because of the accent associated with his speech? Could an employer not hire an individual based on the way he speaks the English language?

Legally speaking, I'm not sure that issue has ever been tested in court, but that is probably something that happens more often than most of us would ever suspect. Perhaps it has even happened to you. Have you ever felt you were excluded from the short list of candidates or actually not hired because of your speech and speech patterns?

If you have been the victim of this type of hiring practice, then you've no doubt walked out of the office depressed and angry, to name but a few emotions. You know you have to keep looking, but your chest tightens just thinking about going through the interview ordeal and hiring process again.

That being said, you've got to be realistic about your accent as well. Some positions require public speaking. Some even require speaking with no identifiable accent. For example, listen to all the national news correspondents. What type of accent do you hear?

None. Normally a news reporter doesn't even have an American regional accent. Many of the native English speakers take elocution lessons to learn how to speak without an accent. Consider the actor who plays the lead in the now-defunct television series, House. What kind of accent does he speak with? If you can't detect an identifiable accent, you're right.

But have you ever heard him on national talk shows? He speaks with a definitive English accent. Which is natural, since he was born in Oxford, English. He's only one of many actors and actresses who can slip in and out of accents seemingly with ease.

Granted, you may not hunger to be an actor and news reporting may not be your profession. Consider the typical business positions, though. Many of these require you to stand up and speak to a group of potential investors or clients or even your colleagues. As with the individual you initially hired you, they're trying not to prejudge you based solely on your accent.

If your accent is so thick that you're spending more time repeating and explaining yourself than concentrating on your method that doesn't forebode well. At this point, your thoughts may be turning negative. "Will I ever find a job at this rate?" you're asking yourself.

You've heard the saying before. "If you keep doing what you've always been doing, you're always going to get what you've always got."

Not eloquent. But true. So how does this pertain to you? Perhaps it's time to take the first steps to change that accent?

No, it won't be easy, even linguists admit this. Listen to what Dianne Markley, a professor at the University of North Texas at Denton, says about learning a second language later in life like you did.

"It's nearly impossible to speak any acquired later in life without an accent." The kicker in this scenario is the research she's unearthed in her academic research. There exists "an incredibly strong statistical correlation between judging someone as cultured, intelligent, and competent and placing them into prestigious jobs" based on the *lack of an accent.*

Many Americans are guilty of this when it comes to their fellow countrymen. While it's not very popular to admit of late, you'd be astonished to discover what some northerners think of those who speak with a dialect normally associated with the south, especially with West Virginia and Kentucky. Or perhaps you wouldn't.

Not Really a Conspiracy

Some people may view this as an intentional conspiracy or some subversive racist behavior. But Victor Arias, who is the manager partner of Heidrick and Struggles said that really isn't the case. He's involved in diversity practices for the executive search firm.

Instead, accents tend to trigger emotions in a subtle way. These emotions, he said, "may make a difference." It's clear he admits that "people "make judgments based on accents."

This doesn't mean these near-instant judgments are all negative, Arias added. But, this is where the idea of discrimination may appear. "Not only may someone with a Hispanic accent may be perceived as less educated," he said. "An individual with a British accent may be seen as "more intelligent." This occurs daily, despite the fact there's absolutely nothing to base this judgment on except the opinion of the person listening.

But that's only the tip of the iceberg. What if someone was interviewed for a job who spoke with an Asian accent? How would that affect his or her chances of winning the position?

Marley explains an Asian accept could be the edge that candidate needed if he or she were interviewing at a scientific or engineering firm. She concluded that these issues aren't set in stone. "They're all very situational."

Even the intensity of the accent triggers certain feelings. Arias readily admits that someone with only a slight accent may be seen by many "as more educated or worldly than someone with a thick accent."

He continues. "I've fallen for that," he said. He has heard both the thick and thin accent and made a rash judgment. He concluded the person's level of education based on hearing him talk and later admonished himself for jumping to that conclusion.

Before we go any further, let's get one thing straight. An accent is nothing more than a pattern of pronunciation. It's in no way a reflection of how well the person uses language. He may speak with a thick accent and speak impeccable English. Despite this, to the native speaker's ear, he may be perceived as an individual who cannot adequately fill the position for which he's applying.

No one is defending this behavior, especially those in charge of doing the hiring. Indeed, candidate – all candidates – should be chosen on their qualifications and only that. But that's not always the case.

Do you recall earlier in this chapter we asked if denying a person a position based on his accent were legal? Apparently it is. Marley uses the position of a customer service representative as a prime example. One of the prime requirements for this position, she explains, is that the candidate has excellent communication skills. An individual who could not be well understood over the phone could very well disrupt the flow of business.

Again, though, this is only the tip of the iceberg, Markley explains. When an employer denies a candidate the position as an excuse to discriminate against his national original, then that's definitely illegal. Take the case of two candidates for the same position. One candidate has a thick Hispanic accent; the other possesses an equally thick French accent.

An employer can't choose the candidate with the French accent over the other based solely on his pattern of speech. That, in effect, would be discrimination.

As you can see, that when you interview for a job, regardless of how qualified you may be, you may be at the mercy of the person doing the hiring more so than an individual who speaks English as his first language.

Once again, we repeat. No one said that was fair. In fairness to those who do the hiring, for the most part, these persons try hard to ignore these aspects. There's also much on the line for them as well. There's a lesson to be learned here for the person doing the hiring. He needs to be aware of the possibility of an unintended and certainly unconscious bias against those who speak with foreign accents.

But there are definitely lessons for those who speak with the accent to learn. Believe it or not, an accent does serve a purpose. One of the most important things it does is connect you and your family with a specific part of the world. In short, it's part of your heritage. Viewed from this perspective, an accent is not a negative thing.

Going for the Interview

Why, of course, you need to interview for your dream job despite your accent. You can't just wring your hands and complain, "Poor me!" You've already got enough stress working when you're job searching. When you do step into that office for the interview and the door closes behind you, keep these few simple rules in mind.

First, use your best grammar. That alone will set you apart from many of the candidates. Don't worry, your use of proper grammar practices will be heard above your accent, regardless of how strong you believe it is.

The second rule is to speak slowly. This allows your interviewer to process your words easier. Not only that, but it forces you to pay attention to your pronunciation. In many ways, you and the interviewer can reach a happy medium.

Whatever else you do, don't get frustrated if you're asked to repeat yourself. It's not the end of the world. How you handle your language and accent under pressure like that has the potential to impress your potential employer. He or she may decide that based solely on your ability to remain calm under stress, you're just the person they're searching for.

But the best advice of all comes from Carlos Soto, who in his capacity as president of the National Hispanic Corporate Council adds this piece of advice as well. "Prepare." Prepare more than any other candidate.

Part of that preparation, he says is to practice your potential answers in English.

Of course, your accent shouldn't make a difference in the hiring process. Unfortunately, it does. That means you should do everything within your power to stack the odds in your favor.

In the next chapter, I suggest that the best starting place to speak more like a native is to understand and concentrate on changing where you put stress or emphasis in your words and sentences. This one step will help you in ways you couldn't even imagine right now.

Chapter 2: Can you Hear That? Placing Stress on the Proper Syllables

It seems like such a subtle aspect – the syllables that Americans stress when speaking. Who would believe that this small point can distinguish a native speaker from one who isn't?

The fact is when you already have to learn the meanings of the words swirling around you and sentence structure and the crazy and not extremely constant rules of English grammar, you're already feeling overwhelmed. Worrying about which syllables to stress when speaking out loud is probably the last thing you're concerned about.

Now, though, you're a more advanced English speaker, so advanced that you're using the English language in many different settings. One of these setting is in your workplace. You now can take a breather because you're fluent in the language.

Your focus is on advancing in your career but, you realize that the biggest roadblock you're encountering is your "foreign accent." It's time to start learning what you can do to reduce that accent.

Your first step is to listen to native speakers with an ear toward which syllable is stressed when words contain more than one syllable. Though I'm a native speaker of English, I noticed the differences in this area when I talked with foreign students who learned British English overseas. I'll never forget the first word I heard from an instructor with an accent. The word was "distribute." As a native speaker I've naturally stressed the second syllable. This instructor though stressed the last syllable. This one subtle difference spoke volumes to me.

For some people reducing their accent, this could easily mean just changing the syllable stressing of many of the words you're using. If you could do this – and only this -- you may be taking a large stride toward eliminating your accent.

It's not Always the First

Probably the biggest mistake those who learn English as a second language make is assuming that Americans naturally – and always – place the spoken emphasis of a two-syllable word on the first syllable. That just isn't so.

Granted, the stressed first syllable occurs quite a bit in the English language, but it just doesn't show up in every single word.

Speak the following list of words out loud. Listen to yourself closely as you say them.

- Window
- Target
- Baby
- Auto

If you've said them as most Americans do, then the first syllable is emphasized. Take just a moment now and say them again, this time ensuring you're placing the stress on the first syllable of each word.

If you have a really good ear, you'll also hear that when you stress the first syllable the pitch of your voice lowers even while you're still speaking it. If you're near a friend you feel comfortable with right now, ask him or her to say these words while you listen attentively. You may even ask him to listen to you while you say these words. Get his feedback.

If you're having a difficult time conquering this, don't worry. In nearly every other language in the world, the stressed syllable is normally pronounced with a rise in pitch. With enough attention to detail and enough practice, you'll soon be able to do this.

Words with Three or more Syllables

The other mistaken assumption many non-native English speakers make is assuming that all words are spoken emphasizing the first syllable. Nothing could be further from the truth.

Speak these words while emphasizing the underlined syllable
- In tro *duce*
- Dis ap *point*
- En ter *tain*

I wish I can provide you with a quick and easy rule of thumb that makes it easy to recognize which multi-syllabic words are pronounced with a distinct stress pattern. Unfortunately, there are no rules. So it's a matter of listening, learning and repeating. Here again, the more you listen and repeat the words, the easier and more natural you'll become when speaking.

Noun versus Verb: Oh, the Stress!

That's all well and good you say. You can concentrate on that. But you also need to know that the syllable being emphasized depends, believe it or not, whether the word is being used as a noun or a verb within the sentence. In essence, how you pronounce the word is dependent on the context in which it's being used. Emphasizing the wrong syllable here also reveals your accent.

You've probably encountered more than your fair share of words that are used as both nouns and verbs. These words are spelled the same, but when used as a noun the stress falls on one syllable. When used as a verb, a different syllable should be stressed. This is more than just a lesson in semantics. Placing the emphasis on the wrong syllable depending on its use actually gives the word an entirely different meaning.

As a rule of thumb, when the first syllable is emphasized you can be fairly confident the word is being used as a noun. If you detect the second syllable is emphasized then you can be relatively sure the word is being used as a verb. If you place the emphasis on the "wrong" syllable, then you may very well be changing the entire meaning of the word without knowing it. Listen to yourself closely as you say the following two sentences out loud. Better yet, if you have a native-English speaking friend recite these out loud. Listen to see if you can tell on which syllable the emphasis is placed.

Your *conduct* was outrageous.
Rick and Jane will *conduct* the meeting.

In the first sentence, the initial syllable of the word conduct is emphasized. In the second example, the second syllable is stressed. Is there really a difference in meaning between the two pronunciations?

Indeed, there is. The noun means how a person acts. The verb means to take charge of or to direct a group of individuals. If you emphasize the wrong syllable of the word when you use it in a sentence, you may not only confuse yourself, but others as well. The following words are those that also fall into this category – two different ways of pronouncing the same word which gives that word two separate meanings.

- Contract
- Suspect
- Insert
- Subject
- Insert

Looking Within: the Sentence that is!

There's yet another way to reduce your accent and sound more like a native speaker. That's by knowing which words to stress within the sentence itself. Again, this is not just some silly rule, even though you may think so. The words you choose to emphasise in a sentence has the potential to change the meaning of the sentence.

When spoken, the English language indicates stress by pronouncing a word or a phrase either slightly louder or longer (or sometimes both). You may also be able to indicate emphasis within a sentence by changing your pitch of certain words.

You need to realize, though, that we aren't talking about altering the stress of the syllables of the words. This requires simply changing the stress of the words in the sentence.

The following is a single sentence to give you an example of how changing the emphasis of one of the words in the sentence can give it a different connotation. Let's use the following sentence as an example.

Rose bought a gorgeous outfit.

When you say this sentence with the word Rose emphasized, **Rose** bought a gorgeous outfit, you're defining who did the buying. It was Rose, not Mary or Jan.

Rose **bought** a gorgeous outfit.

When you place the emphasis on the word bought, you're making sure your listeners know that Rose purchased the dress, it was not given to her (or she stole it!).

If you've really never thought of this before, you may be a bit puzzled now. While there are many rules in the English language and many exceptions as well, there is one dealing with the emphasis on words within sentences that you can usually follow with confidence.

For the most part, native speakers tend to emphasize content words, not the function words. Content words are readily recognizable: nouns, verbs, adjectives, and adverbs. On the other hand, function words are those that are considered parts of speech articles, prepositions, and conjunctions. The second category of words isn't usually emphasized since they're considered transition words.

As transition words, they don't carry the vital information the content words do.

Another way of emphasizing your speech which will help reduce your accent is studying the category of words known as compound words. This is a word created by placing two words with separate meanings together to form one word with a more specific meaning. Think of the word "bathtub."

In English, the word bath is a noun with a meaning of its own and the word "tub" has a meaning and can be used in many situations. When you place these two words together, you get a specific meaning.

So which word do you stress within that compound word? Again, for the most part, the first word of that compound word is emphasized. Below are just several compound words in which the first word is stressed. Read the list below out loud. Be sure to emphasize the first word when you read these:

- Thunderstorm
- Birthday
- Cupcake
- Toothbrush
- Earthquake

The sooner you start putting these rules on emphasis and stress into action, the sooner you'll be on the road to reducing that accent.

Do you know what that means? The sooner you're on the road to opening new and exciting doors in your career. Knowing which syllables to emphasise when speaking is only part of the knowledge needed (and to be implemented). There are still a few hints that can carry you even farther in your quest to reduce your accent. The next section introduces you to these.

Syllables: Still More Secrets to Reveal

Shh! There are still two more secrets native English speakers know that you may not be aware of regarding proper emphasis on words. If you're not aware of these "secrets" you may find you'll never be spot on when it comes to sounding like a native.

Don't get upset. These native speakers aren't deliberating keeping these secrets from you. The truth is that they probably don't even know they exist. I venture to go one step further and claim they probably don't even know what they're doing. They couldn't reveal these secrets even if they wanted to.

We'll talk first about the "ing" sound you see at the end of many English words. When a word ends with a combination of these letters, it's safe to say the emphasis is not on the last syllable. For example, say the word "trying." You'll notice that only the first syllable is stressed. If you can't hear it when you speak it, ask someone else to say this word out loud and listen to it carefully.

Here's a word with even more syllable that follows this rule: demonstrating. Native English speakers only stress the first syllable. You'll find a similar pattern in the word *negotiating.* Only in this word, you'll stress the second syllable, the "go" sound.

This is a rule you can take to the bank. The only exception, of course, (Let's face it, this is English. You'd be disappointed if there weren't any exceptions.) refers to single-syllable words ending in the "ing" sound, like "sing," "fling," or "sting."

When Words End in "ion"

Here's another fairly solid rule of pronunciation. It's based on the "ion" that you've no doubt have come across. You can be sure that the stressed syllable isn't the "ion" ending, rather it's on the syllable directly before it. Even in pronouncing seemingly smaller words the rule still holds up. It works for the word, union, for example as well as the two-syllable word million.

Let's look at the word negotiation. Even though the "ion" sound is pronounced differently (like "shun"), you're still not emphasizing the "ion" sound. You are, however, stressing two other syllables in negotiation.

The next step in your accent reduction program is to learn how native speakers use the vowel sounds: a, e, i, o, and u. Follow me to the next chapter to discover how.

Chapter 3: Learning the Sounds of the Vowels

A, E, I, O, U.

This chapter explains in simple language how to properly pronounce the vowels in order to reduce your accent.

One of the very first aspects of the English language you learned, no doubt, was the differences in sounds between the consonants and vowels. The vowels, of course, are a, e, i, o, and u. How you develop the pronunciation of these five letters will determine your ability to speak like a native.

It would be great if I could tell you that those five vowels contain only five separate and distinct sounds. The truth is though, as you're well aware of, that's just not the truth. There's not only several pronunciations of each of those five vowels, but depending on what syllable you stress in a word, you'll discover yet one more variation of how to pronounce it.

If it sounds messy . . . well, it is. But at the same time, messy isn't quite the same thing as hard. And messy doesn't mean it's not worth tidying the mess up a bit and buckling down and learning and practicing the difference in the spoken word – especially when it's instrumental in losing your accent.

If you recall, we've already talked about how the stressed sounds of English are pronounced. Unlike many languages, those words or syllables that are stressed are, for the most part descend in pitch. You only have to pronounce the vowels to get a good idea of what I mean. Why not say them out loud (You're exempt from this suggestion if you're in a library or other quiet area. Then that suggestion is problematic.)

- A
- E
- I
- O
- U

As you say these out loud, listen closely to how each of these actually does descend in pitch. You could also ask a native speaker, whom you trust to say them out loud. Listen closely to see if you can detect a difference in your pronunciation from his. This might be a part of your accent reduction program that you may need to hone to perfection.

As part of this process, you should also study some of the following sentences we've created to serve as examples and training your pronunciation of the spoken word. Keep in mind that all of the emphasized the sounds your voice should naturally be lowered in pitch. I've italicized the words which need to be emphasized and the pitch lowered.

Let's Start with A

Since it's the first letter of the alphabet it seems the logical place to start. The first thing you should know about this sound is that it actually takes two steps in order to pronounce it accurately.

You begin by pushing your tongue forward in the mouth and then as you're closing your jaw, you move the body of your tong upward until it almost reaches the tooth ridge. At the same time, the sides of the tongue touch the top teeth as you finish enunciating the sound.

Here are a few sentences to get you started.

His secret is *safe* with me.
You, madam, are no *lady.*
Don't you dare *take* advantage of me!
You'll probably need a *safety* net if you insist on doing that.
This marks a big *change* for me.
Maybe she should *make* more cookies?
The pie crust needs to be *flaky.*
Maybe I should *name* the actress' *age.*

EEK!: Listening to the Long E Sound

When you're pronouncing the English long "e" sound properly, you'll immediately notice the sound actually resonates slightly off your lower teeth, as a bright, sharp sound.

In order to pronounce this sound correctly, your tongue should be positioned toward the front of your mouth. In fact, the body of the tongue should be close to the tooth ridge. Ensure that the tongue is higher in the mouth than for the other vowel sounds. You'll notice that this tongue position nearly automatically closes the jaw. The sides of your tongue should touch the top side teeth while you're enunciating this vowel.

You can practice making this sound by repeating out loud any or all of the following sentences. The italicized words should be pronounced as a long "e" sound.

Keep the *keys.*
I don't *need* to *read* it.
They are *meeting* by the oak *tree.*
It's human nature to thirst for *freedom.*
She was *relieved* to *clean* the mess.

If you believe you're struggling with this sound, then ask a trusted friend to read these sentences out loud to you. You can pantomime the words while she's enunciating them or repeat them after her – or both.

In order to make the most progress, you may want to work in a "safe" environment – with a friend who's only concerned with your ultimate progress.

Listen to the Long I Sound

What exactly are you listening for? Technically, this sound is composed of two separate sounds that end with a brief "y" sound. The first step in pronouncing this vowel is to place the tongue within the mouth so it touches the bottom side teeth.

Once you've learned that, then you close the jaw slightly, while the body of the tongue moves upward until it nearly touches the tooth ridge. Again, this position should remind you of the position of the "y" sound. The sides of the tongue, near the front, actually should touch inside of the top, side teeth.

You can hear the long "I" clearly in the following words: guy, invite, sign surprise, while, why. Here are some sentences below you can repeat saying as examples:

She's *trying* to do what is *right.*

Good *night,* sweet prince!
My mother never *liked* that *kind* of talk.
He's a *fine* man.

Look for a new *kind* of *society* to emerge.

Notice that some of these sentences contain more than one long "i" sound. You must pronounce each sound the same way. This is a sure method to temper your accent and sound more like a native speaker.

As you begin practicing you'll probably need to consciously make an effort to pronounce them. You may want to start by repeating these sentences and others you find as you read or hear others talk. The more you use this sound, more comfortable you'll be with it. By the way, in the final chapter of this book are tips to help you put all these ideas into implementation as you work toward your goal.

Oh, No! The Long O Sound

Carefully notice the next time you say a word containing the long "o" vowel. When properly spoken your lips will form a "w" at the end of the word. If you ever find it necessary to seek a word with this sound in a dictionary, you may notice that the reference book even adds the "w" at the end of the pronunciation.

In order to perfect your enunciation of words containing this sound, practice reading out loud either while you're alone or with a native English speaker. You may even want to have your friend read out loud first and then you parrot enunciating his words.

The following sentences all contain at least one word with the long "o" vowel.
I *hope* to go *home* Saturday.
Jane *rowed* the *boat over* to us.
Fred called *home.*
He had *hoped* his parents would *loan* him the money.

The only way to master this sound is to repeat it – as much as possible. By now this advice shouldn't come as much of a surprise: enlist the help of a friend you can trust, or use the internet or television.

The key is to pause the recordings and repeat them. In this way, you can see how close you can sound to the native speaker as possible.

The Long U Sound

The long U sound may be difficult to notice in the written language, but you'll have no trouble identifying it when you hear it. If, however, you're having difficulty pronouncing it like a native speaker, take your time and try to follow these instructions.

Begin with your jaw mostly closed. At the same time, place the top of your tongue close to your tooth ridge. From here, the sound changes into the "oo" sound we've mentioned previously.

You'll form this by performing two acts, one closely behind the other. First, close the lips forming a small circle. Immediately after that, you're lowering the tip of your tongue while raising the back of the tongue.

It's difficult sometimes to recognize when to pronounce the long "u" simply by looking at the spelling of a word. The spelling varies greatly word by word.

The following list of the sentence should help you recognize when the long "u" is spoken.
Of course, the best way to learn this is through repetition.
Here's the list:
My *shoes* are dirty.
I've lost my *toothbrush.*
The same *rules* hold *true* for you, *too.*
He was *introduced* to the largest *opportunity* of his career.
The *community* restricted the developer's plan.
The plan failed to receive the *approval* of city council.
What's the *use?*
Should we really be *doing* this?

If you've been practicing the suggestions and hints found in the previous chapters, then you can be assured you're well on your way of reducing your accent. But, there are still more methods you can learn to eliminate your accent. One of the ways is to learn about the soft palate. It's possible you may have never heard of this portion of your mouth.

If you are familiar with it, it's now time to reveal how to use it properly in order to get you one step closer to your dream job. Follow me to the next chapter.

Chapter 4: Considering the Soft Palate

You probably have heard of the soft palate, even though you may not know exactly what it is or even where it's located.

In simplest terms, it's the delicate piece of cartilage located between the roof of the mouth and what's known as the uvula. That's the fleshy extension that hangs in the back of your mouth.

If you're curious enough, you can place your finger in your mouth, touch your top teeth, then reach back a bit more. Now, you should be able to touch the gum. Don't stop here, though. Continue to reach up and back, past the roof of your mouth. You'll notice it feels a bit wetter and softer, the further back you go.

Congratulations! You've found your soft palate. Now, forget you even have it. Well, almost forget. This portion of your anatomy is the key factor why your voice may sound "nasal" when you speak. That nasal sound, in turn, may be causing your accent to be heavier than it needs to be.

That's because the palate is responsible for separating the oral cavity from the nasal cavity.

When you lower the soft palate, you allow air to pass through the nose via the nasal cavity. This causes you speak with a nasality – or a distinct nasal sound. If, though, the soft palate, remains in the original position, in which it would separate the nasal cavity from the oral cavity, air is trapped. In simple terms, the air can't travel through the nose.

If not the nose, where?

Instead of going up the nose, the air goes up through your mouth. This means you're producing a sound that's not nasal – as not as strong a nasal sound as when the soft palate is lowered.

It only seems logical that enunciating weaker vowel sounds would have the sounds traveling up the back of the throat and closer to the nasal cavity. This adds to the nasality of the sounds. Stop and think for a moment, if you will, where your vocal folds are located: They are positioned toward the front, close to the bottom of the mouth and in the throat.

When this occurs you're producing a nasal-like quality when you speak. You're lowering the soft palate during the course of your talking.

The goal is to sound less nasal. In order to do this, you'll want to consciously not lower your soft palate when speaking.

The most efficient way to do this is by speaking more from your throat or at a minimum, speak from the lower part of your mouth. Make a conscious effort not to speak through the upper portion of your mouth.

When you try this, you may be confronted with an Irrefutable law of nature: It seems impossible to speak without moving your soft palate – at least a bit.

Limited Jaw Movement

Before you say "there's nothing I can do to reduce this," I'm going to say, "Yes, there is." When you're not moving your jaw much, you're enunciating less and producing weaker vowel sounds. This could be a large part of your nasal sound which, in turn, contributes to your accent.

Your goal should be to produce vowel sounds that are stronger. In order to do this, you'll need to enunciate more clearly. You'll discover you'll have to work harder to produce the sound by moving your mouth and lips. As you do all of this, you'll be speaking with more definition. This may mean you'll need to adopt a slower speech pattern.

Speaking slowly general frustrates advanced English students like you. But be patient. It won't be something you'll need to do for a long time. Consider it a temporary trade-off.

Another bone of contention for many individuals who speak English as a second language is that pesky "r" sound. Getting the pronunciation is a bit more difficult than many individuals believe. But it can be accomplished. Visit the next chapter to learn the way to do this.

Chapter 5: Learning about the "R" Sound: It's Trickier than you Think

It's called the hard "r" sound and it's hard in more ways than one. In fact, this sound is even a bit difficult for many native English speakers to conquer. I mentioned in the introduction. I spent at least one year in speech therapy in an attempt to learn the proper pronunciation of that sound.

I eventually conquered the sound, but to this day, if I'm tired, I'll mispronounce it.

Even though it may be tough, many instructors of English feel that the "r" sound is the "most important aspect of the American accent." No pressure here, now is there, to get this right?

You might also be interested in knowing that the hard American "r" is actually the only "r" worldwide that is distinctly considered a true hard sound. Yes, the Irish sound "aaR" comes in a close second.

In order to make this sound correctly, you'll move the tip of your tongue toward the back of your mouth, pointing it backward and flex it.

The hard sound comes in three varieties: or, ar, and air.

We'll tackle the "or" sound first. Keep in mind, though, that if you can pronounce one, you'll eventually be able to pronounce all three. Just don't get discouraged. You'll also want to always keep in mind learning how to pronounce the "r" properly will go a long way toward reducing your accent.

Here are just a few examples of words with that "or" sound: floor, for, fork, order, ordinary, force, and remorse.

Of course, this is English so you can bet your bottom dollar that there are exceptions to this variety of spelling. Just a few of these include the word, worm work, world and worst. Another variety of pronunciation can be heard in English as well, which is the "ore" sound. A few good examples of these include before, restored, more and shore.

Surprisingly, the same sound is often found in words spelled with the letter "a." Consider the words – all of these sounds, you'll notice follow the letter "w." These words include: swarm, war, warn, toward, and warrior.

Notice the difference, however, when the "e" follows the "war" sound as in warehouse, hardware and stare.

Yes, this can be a bit confusing. But as you study it more, it'll become second nature to you. The following sentences will all have the hard "r" sound in at least word. If you practice, you will conquer it. Guaranteed.

He placed his *order* with his server.

This is a *world* of *disorder.*

Many interpretations were *explored* in this book.

The *four* of them were searching for the *fork.*

The building looked *ordinary.*

We have *restored* the *floor* to its original elegance.

The *corners* of his mouth twitched.

May the *force* be with you.

Checking out the "ar" Sound

The sound of "ar" is produced, for the most part, when the combination of "a" and "r" are spoken together with no "e." Some of these words are quite simple, including: car, bar, far, Mars, darn, large, dark, arm, smart and remark.

Just when you think you may have found a pattern, the fact that you're studying English hits you square in the face. Here are a few words that are exceptions to the rule: backward, toward and forward.

If all this weren't enough, it's time to throw in one more exception. Take a good look at the word "our." Technically, it would be pronounced so it sounds like the vowel sound in power. But Americans, more frequently pronounce it with the "ar" sound.

Here are a few sentences to help you learn how to perfect this sound.

I'm going to *our* car.

That's *our* only chance to claim what's truly *ours.*

Our meeting starts shortly

He was tall, *dark,* and handsome.

The *art* of writing letters has nearly disappeared.

She *startled* the intruder.

He gave her *harsh* glance.

He's a member of the *armed* services.

Exploring the "Air" Sound

Now that you're busy studying those typically American hard "r" sounds, we're about to move on to a slightly different sound, but still well within the definition of a hard "r." That's the "air" sound.

You'll discover this is more often sounded out like "ar" when it's followed by an "e," "y," or "i." Say these words out loud, or better yet, ask a native English speaker say the following few words out loud to get a better of the idea of what I mean: care, share, scare, scares, barely, marry, rare.

The sound of "air" may show up with other spellings as well, most noticeably "ere" and "ear." Look at the words, wear and swear. Ask a native speaker to pronounce them for you or listen to them on an online dictionary which offers correct pronunciation of its entries. Be careful, though, because there are two common exceptions to this that immediately come to mind: were and ear.

Confusing? You bet. But you'll probably want to study and practice a bit and even enlist the help of native English speaking friends. Listen to someone recite these sentences, then repeat them after him or her.

I don't *care* what you think of me.

Do you know *where* Tony is?

I was *upstairs* most of the day.

I *swear* I don't know *where* she is.

The trick to pronouncing and sound like a native is to remember that all hard "r" sounds are short. Don't linger too long on that sound. Again, if you listen closely to native speakers, you'll at least have an idea of the sound you should be making when speaking these words. Then you can tackle it for yourself.

Chapter 6: Conquering the "th" sound

Just when you think the English language couldn't get much more confusing, we're moving from the hard "r" sound to the "th" sound. This is another aspect of the English language that frequently even gives native speakers a difficult time.

While I was in speech therapy for the "r" sound, my best friend was going through the same instruction, only for the "th" sound.

But, while it may be – dare I say – "foreign" to you, you'll soon be conquering the pronunciation of these two letters just as you have done with all the other tricky sounds we've thrown your way.

In this chapter, we're going to talk about the two subtle, yet different sounds these two letters make depending on the words in which they're included. Linguists refer to the two sounds as either "voiced" or "unvoiced."

The voiced and unvoiced "th" sounds are the only pair that actually uses the same spelling – which, you can undoubtedly guess, only adds to the confusion. This sound is also problematic, because to be truthful, most Americans probably can't tell the difference most of the time. If we were to take the time to truly listen closely enough, we'd be able to detect. Before you're done reading this chapter you'll probably be able to tell the difference yourself. The next natural step then is to embrace the differences and conquer the sounds.

How to Pronounce these Sounds

As we mentioned the differences in sound are subtle. It should come as no surprise then that the way you pronounce them is also very much alike. Below are the basic instructions on how to get started with either sound.

First, you position the tip of your tongue behind the top of your front teeth. This ensures that when you go to pronounce this, you'll have generated the friction necessary for proper enunciation. Keep your lips relaxed.

An Alternative Method

There's also a second way to pronouncing this sound. In this method, you'll position the tip of your tongue between your top and bottom front teeth. If you find yourself using this method, you may also discover it makes it difficult to shift quickly to other sounds.

The reason for this is that your tongue needs to be so far in front when its placed between your upper and lower front teeth. You may not consider this much of a distance, but your tongue doesn't have quite the agility to move swiftly, either.

Consider this: Continuous Consonants

The other hint that is helpful in learning to pronounce either the voiced or unvoiced "th" sound is that they are what is known as "continuous consonants." This means that you should, under ideal conditions, be able to hold these sounds for a few seconds. Not only should you be able to hold them, but do so with an even and smooth enunciation for the entire time. No pressure here, right?

The second aspect of these sounds are they're known as "fricatives," which means most of the sound is derived from the friction produced from the air traveling through that small opening in the vocal tract.

Now that we've had the technicalities of pronouncing these words correctly, it's time to show you the subtle difference between the sounds of the voiced and unvoiced "th."

The Good News about the "the" Sound

After everything you've learned about the "voiced" and "unvoiced" "th" sound, you may be a bit surprised to learn that there is even a spark of good news out there about it. Believe it or not, it's considered one of the most consistent sounds in the English language.

When you see the combination of letters together you can be sure that they are almost always pronounce it the same way. But English being what it is, does contain its exceptions in this sound as well. Consider, for example, the words, Thailand, Thomas and Thames all of which you'll pronounce with a "t" sound.

You'll also find that on occasion that the "th" is really a cluster of two consonants and you'll pronounce the "t" and "h" separately. This occurs most notably in compound words.

Some of these include anthill, lightheaded, lighthouse, and knighthood.

Examples of Voiced "th" Sounds

Here are few examples of the voiced "th" sounds. The voiced option can appear in any part of a word, the front, the middle or the end. I realize that makes it more difficult to recognize. In order to hear the difference and the proper pronunciation, as a native speaker to read these words to you: that, than they, though, themselves, therefore, therein, feather, together, bathing, father, mothing, clothing, weather, another, rather, soothing, tether, breathe, lathe. Seethe, loathe.

Just as with the voiced "th" sound, the unvoiced alternative can and does show up in any part of a word. The following is a list – of course, not complete – of the unvoiced "th" sound. Listen closely to a native speaker say these. Then try to imitate him or her as closely as you can.

They include: thorn, thin, think, thousand, thirsty, thief, thermometer, thaw, thread, thoughtful, three, thick, therapy, thimble, Thursday, bathtub, toothache, toothbrush, toothpaste, toothpick, marathon, python, healthy, truthful, wealthy, athlete, birthday, pathway, cloth, math, math, tooth, month, fifth, path, beneath, path, wreathe, broth, booth

Are You Making any of these Errors?

If the "th" sound is new to you, it may take some practice for you to learn the proper placement of your mouth, as well as listening to the correct sound. The good news is that while this is a difficult sound, there are a few ways that it's sometimes pronounced by non-native speakers. If you can identify one of these ways, then you may find it easier to correct and even perfect your pronunciation.

For the most part, those who speak English as a second language stay within the appropriate sound category. They substitute the voiceless "t" or "s" sounds for the voiceless "th." Similarly, they use the voiced "d" and "z" sounds for the voiced "th." Here are just a few ways these can manifest in your accent.

Many individuals end up saying "mouse" when they're trying to pronounce "mouth." They say the word "tree" for the word "three." They say "sink" for "think" and "bat" for "bath." You'll also hear the word "dare" for "there" and "ladder" for "lather."

If this sounds like you, then you're probably already working on this area. Don't be too upset if the pronunciation doesn't click with you immediately. Work on this area consistently and persistently. You'll be pleasantly pleased – and mildly proud – at how quickly you'll pick it up.

In the meantime, we'll talk about another portion of the English language which may be giving you a difficult time: diphthongs. Don't know what they are? You're not alone. In the next time, you'll discover what they are and how you can use them to speak like a native.

Chapter 7: Discovering Diphthongs

You say you've never heard of the word "diphthong" before? No problem.

Many native speakers have no idea what a diphthong is even though they use them every day. Probably many times throughout the day, in fact. The fact is that it's difficult to speak the English language without using diphthongs.

A diphthong is a single vowel sound that is composed of more than one vowel. It really is much easier to understand than you're thinking at this moment. This sound begins as one vowel sound and moves toward the next sound. When they're pronounced they are enunciated as one sound. Take the words coin for example. Your mouth begins as an "o" but as you form the "i" sound, it's pronounced as "oy."

Loud is also a good example of a diphthong. It, too, starts with an "o" sound, but then merges with the "u" to produce an "ow" sound that rhymes with "wow."

These two pronunciations stand in contrast to two vowels standing together in a word which retain their distinct vowel sounds. Words with these sounds are called monophthongs. The words violin, triage and chaos fall into this category. Notice that not only are the vowels are pronounced separately, but they also are split into separate syllables.

A Difference you can Feel

If you're unsure how you're pronouncing them, there is, believe it or not, a method you can use to test yourself. Place your index finger on both sides of your mouth. Next, say the short vowel sound of "a" (pronounced "ah"). Your fingers shouldn't move. Nothing happens. Why? Your fingers are motionless, because your mouth doesn't move during this. You'll discover this is the case with most of the vowel sounds.

This same test ends with different results when you pronounce the "oy," and "ow" sounds. When you place one index finger on each side of your mouth and make those sounds, your mouth should move. In effect, your mouth moves from making the first vowel sound to the next to create this sound.

Curiously (and I certainly don't mention this to confuse you), there are two other vowel sounds with actually pass the diphthong test. They aren't vowel consonants, but free-standing vowels: the long "i" and "a" sounds. If you place your index fingers on the side of your mouth, you'll discover that your mouth moves – because they are composed of two distinct sounds. Most linguists recognize these as diphthongs. Most reading teachers do not.

Here are a few of words that are pronounced as one sound, blending one vowel sound flawlessly into the other. This short list shows you the diphthong that is pronounced in the words, how and wow.

These include: cow, allow, owl, down, clown, drown, browser, browse, powder, proud, cloud, doubt, foul, noun, south, mouth, couch, found, around, amount, mountain, bounce, allowing, plowing, towel, bowel, hour, sour, flour.

The other diphthong we've mentioned is the "oy" sound as in the word boy. You'll discover that there are many words with these sound, some with different spellings. Here is a partial list -- and I do mean only a partial list: noise, voice, avoid, poison, join, point, foil, oil, spoil, exploit, toy, toying, annoy, employ, employing, employer oyster, destroyer.

Have I filled your head with enough rules and regulations – and exemptions to those same rules and regulations? Are you ready to say, "Enough!"

I have to admit you have enough material to master to take you on your journey to sounding like a native English speaker. In the following chapter, I'm ready to show you how to put it all together. Go ahead! Take a deep breath before you go there. You deserve at least that.

Chapter 8: Putting it All Together

For some individuals, the idea or reducing or eliminating their accent appears like an insurmountable hurdle. Just when you think you can see the light at the end of the tunnel, you encounter a person who's been speaking it as their second language longer than you've been alive. The person is still speaking with an accent. What gives?

If they haven't eliminated their accent by now, how could you ever hope to? First, stop thinking like this. You can and will reduce your accent as long as continue to pursue this goal. Of course, there are some more effective ways and not-so-effective ways. This chapter lists some of the most efficient methods of putting everything you've learned up to this point and literally "putting it all together."

1. Watch television shows

When I talk to individuals how have successfully shed their accent, they confess that watching TV played a major role. Wow! I thought that impressive. I had never really thought of this being a viable option until a variety of people, with different first languages, kept telling me how much watching television helped them.

Why would that be so?

First, watching television is a safe way of studying what the English language is all about. Not only do you get to hear how it's spoken naturally, but you can also sample the idioms used within a safe environment. If you don't understand a phrase or a word you can either literally write it down later to discover the meaning or ask someone later.

Secondly, you'll develop an ear for the nuanced accent of the speaker and how you may then repeat it. If you can watch television shows already pre-recorded on DVDs, so you can listen to them time and again and immerse yourself in the language and especially the accent.

2. National Public Radio as a Model

Perhaps there is no better model for perfecting the pronunciation of the English language that National Public Radio better known NPR. Even native-speaking English speakers are in awe of the powers of speech the typical host and reporter has.

3. Shadowing

This technique is highly recommended if you're either in your beginning stages or for individuals, like yourself, who are already advanced students trying to speak with less of an accent in order to be better accepted at work or within your study group.

If you've never heard of it before, the concept is simple. While you're listening to someone or something, like a television show or a National Public Radio broadcast, try to repeat – technically to shadow – what you've just heard. Do this as quickly as you can. By this, I mean to repeat it sentence by sentence. It doesn't matter if you repeat the entire story. The goal is to pick a sentence, repeat it. Then as soon as you have done that, repeat the next sentence you hear. t is one of the most beneficial ways to learn.

The only addition to this technique is to be walking swiftly while you're doing this. I wish I could answer why the walking and talking – when taken together work so well, but I can't. Many experts believe it may have some relation to receiving more oxygenation helps you to learn.

As a professional attempting to boost his ability to sound like a native speaker, you're probably ready just to jump in at the advanced shadowing. You can shadow an audio recording of a book or even a news talk show while you walk. If you're reading – and you're careful – consider walking and reading. This is problematic at times. But if he stays in your home and walks from room to room where you're comfortable maneuvering, it works nicely.

Those who have used shadowing as a method of acquiring a more American accent when speaking English, say that while it's effective, it's also a tedious, difficult method to accomplish.

I tell you this not to discourage you, but to warn you. The individual described shadowing as a "boring, grueling technique." He also said it was "about as much fun and as much work as weightlifting.

However painstaking this technique may be, he did offer this one bit of advice. Only perform shadowing one sentence at a time. Listen to the sentence; repeat the sentence. Listen to the sentence; repeat the sentence.

After all these caveats, he did admit that he didn't "know of any other effective way to reduce an accent with home study."

Keep in mind that reducing your accent may not always be easy, but if you remember all the reasons you're doing it – which may very well include a promotion or advancement in your career, you'll then realize the effort you exert is well worth.

4. What about Podcasts and YouTube?

There are primarily two ways you can put podcasts and YouTube to work for you in reducing your accent. The first is straightforward. Search the internet for podcasts and YouTube videos created specifically to give you advice on the topic. There are several good varieties. As you search, you'll discover the one that perfectly fits your needs.

The second method and is one frequently overlooked. Listen to a podcast or a YouTube video on a subject you enjoy. In this way, the subject matter will be able to keep your interest. Use these as a form of role modeling. Listen to them not only for content, but to immerse yourself in the English language. Imitate the way the native English-speaking participants talk.

Adopting a Role Model

This probably seems too simple to work. Many individuals have tried it and say that it works much better than they thought it would. This technique is just as it says. Select an individual who speaks English the way you would ideally like to. Be sure when you're searching for this "role model" that you select an individual you can trust.

Part of this exercise is that you're going to ask him or her to correct your English when he notices your accent getting heavier. Ask him if he'll work with you. Sometimes this means stopping an entire conversation and spending a few moments just working on a phrase or a word.

Your responsibility is to follow his instructions. Now you can see why you need to select an individual you can trust. Don't take offense when he corrects you, keeping in mind he's doing exactly what you asked of him.

The following chapter is all about reverse accent mimicry. This method, which is remarkably similar to the ones we've talked about in this chapter, actually takes the suggestions one step further.

To discover how more than one person has successfully reduced his accent using this remarkable imaginative method, all you need to do is to continue on to the next chapter.

Chapter 9: Reverse Accent Mimicry

Since your goal is to reduce your foreign accent, then you may want to explore the concept of *reverse accent mimicry.* It's not the simplest idea to understand, but it just may be an exercise that'll work for you. So I feel compelled to at least talk a bit about it.

The idea is that the quickest and easiest method of breaking through your accent and any pronunciation issues in your second language, in this case, English, is by finding a person who speaks English as their first language and simply mimic their "accent" while you're speaking your own native language.

Think about it for a moment. When I first explored this concept, I had to allow the idea soak in for a while. In fact, when it was first explained to me, I wasn't even sure I fully understood the concept. But as I continued to explore the theory, it made sense to me.

In essence, you'll walk through four steps.

1. Find a "reverse model."

This is a person who speaks your native language with a thick accent based on the language you're attempting to conquer. Let's say your first language is French, but your goal is to speak flawless English. You're looking for someone who is comfortable speaking English but, still has his or her French accent.

I know right now, you're tempted to bail and move on to another chapter, but at this point stay with me, please.

2. Your goal is to mimic your model in your first language.

If you speak French, then ask this person to speak some in French. Don't just repeat what they say, mimic everything you notice in how they speak, down to their gestures. In a very real way parrot everything you can as well as you can about them when they speak.

If you're afraid you won't remember what your model is saying, then give him a monologue to read or a portion of a book to read. If it would make you feel more comfortable record a television show or watch on Netflix or Hulu. You can then just mimic these characters down to a tee.

3. Transition this mimicry into your second language.

The next step is to shift to mimicking this character or person, only this time in the second language. Yes, the language in which you're trying to reduce your accent. It's essential at this point that you keep everything as close to his "act" as possible. Don't change is animation, expression, pronunciation or even intonation. The only difference is that now you're speaking in the language you're learning – your second language. You'll discover that while you were mimicking your model, you almost subconsciously adopted much of the necessary native nuances of the language which are vital to learning a second language.

4. Finally, use one-on-one interaction with a speaker of your second language.

Preferably, you'll want this face-to-face time to be with a native English speaker. As you speak with him, you'll notice an immense reduction in your accent. Not only that, but you'll soon discover that others can hear it in your spoken word as well.

A friend of mine is a strong advocate of this method. His first language is English, but was trying hard to speak French like a native. Unfortunately, as he tells it his "carry-over English foreign accent" always got in the way. He explained that even though his French grammar and vocabulary were great, his listeners "often misunderstood me or asked me to repeat." Sound familiar?

He finally broke through that barrier, he told me, when he was in France watching the old movie Gigi, starring the legendary actor, Maurice Chevalier. The theater showed its original English version with French subtitles. After the movie was over, he began doing his impersonation of Chevalier, mimicking everything from gestures to the way he spoke English.

Without giving it a second thought, he was "effortlessly mimicking French prosodic melody and stress patterns," as he explained it to me. He said what he heard as he did this was his speaking with exaggerated and tenser French speech patterns. Without even knowing it he was using the French intonation and pronunciation qualities that had been so difficult for him to acquire up until then.

Furthermore, he continued to tell me excitedly, that he suddenly had the ability to use "a whole cluster of salient spoken French intonation and pronunciation qualities" that had before somehow eluded him.

Reverse accent mimicry could be a unique and enjoyable, even playful, way to reduce your foreign accent quickly. At the very least, you can give it a try. If nothing else, you'll have a good time. My bet is, though, that you'll find, just as my friend did, it could be the "superhighway" to reducing your accent.

He even confessed to me: "I discovered that from that moment on, my accent problems were nearly gone."

Give it a try. If it doesn't work for you, that's fine. But if it indeed does, then you've found the elusive "superhighway" to accent reduction. Congratulations.

The following chapter provides you with eight tips, tricks, and techniques of squeezing in methods of accent reduction throughout your day. These are, for the most, part quick and easy.

The goal of these is to keep the need of accent reduction front and center in your consciousness. To discover these, simply continue reading to the next chapter.

Chapter: 10: 8 Secrets to Accent Reduction

If you're as serious about reducing your accent as I believe you are, then you're probably already implementing quite a few of the methods explained in the previous chapters. In addition to those, I'd like to share with you eight secrets of accent reduction that most individuals don't think to share with you. It's not that they're purposely keeping these tips, tricks, and techniques from you. It's that they may have stumbled across them in their search for shortcuts to accent reduction.

Test out the following tips. If they work for you great!

1. The English language has a unique cadence.

Some have compared the cadence of English to that of jazz music. Think about how in that genre one note sometimes flows effortlessly into the other and how the intonation of the music changes at a moment's notice.

Many students, new to the English language, are naturally careful in their speech, fearful of making a mistake. They speak slowly and carefully with pauses between every word. This, for a native, is a telltale sign that English isn't your first language. So many English words are connected. Consider the phrase "How are you?" The first two words are said almost as if they were one.

Another good example of this is the phrase "got you." For some reason, native speakers string this together to make it sound like one word. On top of that, they also place a "tch" sound in there. In effect, it sounds more like "gotchya" than anything else.

The point is that if you deliberately separate every word you speak, you'll sound stilted and robotic. The next time when hear someone speak English, pay attention to this aspect of the language.

2. Listen to audiobooks.

Without a doubt, this is one of the best ways to reduce your accent. Not only that, but it's a "safe" method. While you listen to these native speakers in the privacy of your car or home, you'll be able to get the feel for all the nuances that go into the English language. In effect, this secret trains your ear to actually "stop hearing with your accent," which can be critical to your ultimate success.

3. Detect when an "s" is really a "z."

What? There really are times in the English language that we write the word using the letter "s" but end up saying the word as if it were a "z." Go figure.

You'll find this occurs, more often than not, when the "s" is the final letter of the word. Knowing when to use the "z" sound and when not to will help you reduce your accent. Listed below are just a few words illustrating this example.

In the following words, the final "s" sounds like a "z" when spoken: beds, cries, rays. The next three words end in the letter "s" and are pronounced as an "s": bells, hits, tacks.

4. Learn to detect "voiced" sounds from "unvoiced" ones.

Many consonants in the English language are only spoken as voiced. These include, "b," "d," "g," "l," "m," "n," "ng," "r," "v," "w," "y," and "z." Quite a long list, isn't it?

We've talked about this in regard to the "th" sound, which has a slight difference to its sound whether it's voiced or unvoiced. What we didn't mention, however, is the fact that there are a few others, including the "h," "k," "p," "t," "s."

Here's another way to tell whether the words below have a voiced or unvoiced consonant. Place your index and middle fingers at the hollow of your neck. The closer to the base of the neck you can put it, the more accurate you'll be at identifying the sound. If the sound is voiced, there'll be no vibration there. If you do feel a vibration then you'll know the sound is unvoiced.

In each pair of words, one is voiced and the other not. Practice distinguishing one from the other:

bad/bat	rod/rot
lab/lap	tab/tap
bag/back	beg/beck
bus/buzz	lace/laze

5. Record yourself speaking English.

Yes, record yourself, but don't stop there. Take a sentence or two and record yourself. Then play it back and write down what you said. Here's the catch, though, don't write it as it's correctly spelled. Transcribe it phonetically. Let's say you recorded yourself speaking the sentence: "I think the bed is too soft." What you hear when you transcribe this is "I dink da bet iss doo sof."

If that's what you hear, write it down. Look for errors. In this example, we know the "th" sound came out as a "d" and the voiced sounded more like a voiceless "t." Additionally, the "z" sound in the word is sounded more like an "s" and the final "t" in soft was actually dropped.

This is one of the best ways that you can evaluate yourself. Of course, the key is to keep using this method while at the same time listen to native speakers to help you overcome these errors.

6. Buy a Pronunciation Dictionary

This can be one of the most valuable things you can do. If you've never heard of one before, it's exactly what it sounds like. In addition to giving you the proper pronunciation, this type of dictionary also helps you with discovering the proper stress and how to break the word into syllables.

You can find them in just about any bookstore. If you have trouble finding it, ask a clerk; she'll know exactly what you mean. Some varieties of this dictionary may even come with an audio CD so you can easily listen to the correct pronunciations.

7. Practice, practice, practice.

Perhaps this secret isn't quite what you expected. It will, however, make the difference between speaking with or without an accent. The fact is that unless you use the English language, you'll never be able to speak it without your native accent. Give yourself time to learn the pronunciation. Don't think that you'll lose your accent overnight. If you practice, though, you will eventually speak more like a native.

This happens, if for no other reason, you're practicing the correct placement and movement of your tongue.

8. Learn the art of message chunking

The art of what?

I can hear you ask that now. It's called message chunking and it's a habit many native English speakers have. To sound truly native, your delivery of English need to be broken into "clear and logical" breaks of words, commonly called chunks. These are often referred to as thought groups.

In English, an average thought group is approximately three to four words long. At the end of each of these thought groups, native English speakers insert a pause. It's only a split second long, but if you listen close enough you can hear it. They're called thought groups because they are a chunk of words that can stand alone and still make sense. They're similar to a short portion of a much longer sentence. If you choose the wrong time to pause, like in the midst of one of these thought groups, you'll discover your listeners have a difficult time following your train of thought.

Not only that, but within each of these chunks of thoughts, there should be a single word that takes on the main emphasis. This is the word that needs to be stressed or emphasized when you speak. It may take a while to discover exactly where to stop to create these chunks of messages. With enough practice, though, you'll soon know nearly instinctively how to create effective and intelligent thought groups.

You may not think this is a big deal, but give it a try. You'll be surprised at how much your accent disappears.

Even if you only implement a few of these eight tips, you'll be making great strides in reducing your accent. When you put these tips together with the previous suggestions and directions found in all the other chapters, you've found a remarkable and nearly unbeatable road to sounding more like a native speaker of an English daily.

Conclusion

Congratulations! You have learned the most important tools needed to effectively reduce your foreign language and make great strides in acquiring one that sounds more closely to a native English speaker.

Having said that, I'm sure you realize you probably haven't mastered any of these techniques – yet, that is! – nor do you sound like you have spoken English since the day you were born.

But, if you continue to study these, practice them on a daily basis and keep some of these tips, tricks, and techniques in your consciousness, then you've taken some of the most important steps toward making it so.

If prior to reading this book, you felt as if there were no hope for you in ever accomplishing this, then my sincere desire is that we've lifted your expectations that it really is possible to do so. You've heard many people from other countries talk fluently and flawlessly in English – without the accent. If they can do it, so can you.

You'll naturally want to re-read certain sections of this book, depending on what presents the most trouble for you. I encourage you to. In this way you can work on the most stubborn aspects you're encountering.

There are plenty of methods other than what I've just presented here. These, though, I've discovered are among the quickest and most relevant one. I'm quite sure you'll find more ways to do this than what I could list here. If so that's great. Just keep in mind that for the most part, you'll want to listen carefully to those who were raised in English as their first language.

If you're planning on being successful, you'll have to put yourself on the line at times and ask those native-speaking individuals you know to help you overcome your accent. You'll discover that there are many people who would not only be glad to help you in your quest, but would probably be honored as well.

A Tedious Job

I've quoted one friend who described overcoming his accent as being as tedious and boring as lifting weights. For some that may be so. Keeping this in mind, try to meet this goal with a smile, knowing that in the end, all the effort and "weightlifting" is worth it. Because it is.

There's not a place or sentence in this book in which I've promised shedding your accent and adopting one closer to a native speaker of English would be easy. You, however, already knew that. If it were easy, you wouldn't need any guidebook.

So as much as you dream of waking up one day and waving a magic wand that allows you to speak perfect English accent-free, it's not going to happen that way. It will, however, occur and with less pain than you may think, when you develop the habit of speaking English and listening to native speakers on a daily basis.

Don't worry that you may not be able to learn it in person. Take your education whichever way works. By this, I mean that the internet opens new vistas generations prior to us never had.

In previous generations, meeting native speaking individuals of a language were about the only way to shed your own accent. You had to be lucky enough to visit the country or happen to run into one in your country.

Today, you can turn on the television, cruise the internet, watch Netflix and so much more. Many of them, by the way, can be accomplished in a "safe" environment – one in which you needn't fear about anyone making light or teasing you about your accent.

It's up to you to take advantage of these amazing methods as best you can.

Continue working toward your goal. The sky's the limit.

Public Speaking Secrets

How to Deliver a Perfect Presentation as a Foreign
Professional

Whitney Nelson

Contents

Introduction

Milosh knew one thing for sure: That making this presentation was essential to his eventual rise in the company. Okay, Milosh knew something else. He knew he wanted nothing more than to make a name in the company. He wanted a promotion and he wanted a pay raise. The presentation, scheduled for several weeks from now, was a large part of attaining his goals.

He sat down with his former English teacher and expressed his concerns. His main fear was that because he didn't speak English like a native, he faced a larger chance of failure.

When he confided his fears to his English teacher, he laughed. "Milosh, I'll be straight up with you," he said. You're one of the most talented students I've ever had. You'll give that presentation and nail it." "

But before parting, his teacher did speak a bit on the extra burdens that foreign professionals encounter when they're facing an audience. This information isn't meant to make you feel more inadequate, it's meant to encourage you to prepare. It's meant to emphasize the importance of proper preparation.

Ask any foreign professionals. They'll all tell you the same thing. Sure, native speakers may whine about stage fright and forgetting their presentation, but this situation is doubly as difficult for anyone who's speaking to a large audience in English as their second language.

It's only natural for it to be a bit more difficult, just a tad more problematic, a little more challenging. That doesn't mean it's impossible or, for that matter, you won't find it one of the more thrilling times of your life. For many, it truly is.

It might be more satisfying for the average ESL (English as Second Language) they've faced all the possible hurdles. They've seriously prepared for them and conquered them all. They discover two things. First, they've raised their self-confidence levels which help them realize that there are other goals they now could embrace.

Secondly, they do have a place in corporate America. They can communicate just as well as their native-speaking peers and they're ready to compete, anywhere and anytime.

Foreign Professionals and Additional Presentation Concerns

Let's face it. Public speaking may strike fear and anxiety in those who are just beginning, regardless of what language they grew up speaking. When you add in a dash of fear based on culture shock and excessive concern about speaking the language well enough to be understood by a group of your peers and colleagues, even the best of students may be a bit intimidated.

According to some experts, the level of anxiety you'll experience is increased compared to native speakers. This makes sense to many since you're not only concerned about the writing and structure of your presentation, but you have additional apprehensions that a native speaker wouldn't have. For one thing, you may be wondering if your audience can understand you, given your accent.

Those students who learn through more visual means are those who seem to be more hesitant and more troubled when told they must present their findings to others. If this describes you, don't resign yourself to a mediocre presentation. Yes, you can give your audience an outstanding talk, opening it up to audience participation without breaking a sweat.

Even accounting for the potential of cultural indifference, you can be more self-confident and in turn, present a better talk than even your native speaking counterpart.

How do I know? Because I see it occur every day. If even one ESL professional can give not just a good presentation, but an excellent speech, then you can too. Keep that in mind.

Some call it Communication Anxiety

Just like with other students, you may be suffering from communication anxiety. How can you tell if your fear is unnaturally high and are in need of a bit more specialized and generalized practice before you stand in front of your audience?

Trust me, you'll know. You won't have to take any quizzes or ask anyone. If you feel unusually nervous, then do yourself a favor and begin to take the necessary steps to practice. And do it immediately.

In this way, you'll feel infinitely more comfortable with just the idea of giving the speech. You probably won't be feeling be totally fear-free, but you'll discover an underlying feeling of self-confidence you didn't possess before your practice.

How Can This Book Help You?

This book is your valuable companion as you're practicing for your next presentation in English. Regardless of what your native tongue is, you'll discover these universal suggestions, practice exercises and secrets you probably never knew existed to be of amazing help.

For example, in the first chapter, we've outlined the **four major fears** of any speaker whose first language is not English when they face the audience. In addition to the natural fears, we'll also tell you the first steps in overcoming them.

A large part of feeling confident when you walk to the podium and begin to talk is to be prepared. That's why many of the ideas and concepts in this book fall into this category. Illustrating this idea is the second chapter, which will not only encourage you to practice your English prior to speaking in public, but provide you a few of the more successful methods others in your position have used successfully.

Chapter three speaks more generally to the equipment you need for a great presentation. Of course, these are undoubtedly the same tools any great speaker needs. But when you're fighting off an extra level of fear because you're speaking in your second language, it's even more important that you don't run into any technical or electronical problems that can shake your confidence. There are times when one unexpected hurdle can cast a pall over the rest of your speech – if you allow it. The more prepared you are and the more comfortable in operating your equipment, the smoother the presentation will flow.

Have you considered how to build a rapport with your audience? That's the topic of the following chapter. The best speakers know how to make the audience feel as if they're speaking specifically to them – that what they have to say was written just for them, in fact. In many ways, that's the truth.

Regardless of where your abilities lie on the English-speaking spectrum, believe me, your English is great if you're already making a presentation. Among other concepts you'll encounter in this portion of the book include speaking in simple terms and using clear prose. Accomplishing this may mean a bit of work on your part. You may have to break through some of the technical jargon or vocabulary of your area and make it sound more user-friendly to your audience.

The last thing you want is your listeners losing valuable information, not because they couldn't understand your English, but they couldn't understand the vocabulary of your area of interest.

Signposting is Essential

Chapter Six is all about signposting. If you can learn to help guide your listeners through your talk – even before you've gone into much detail – then you're making it that much easier for them to follow your train of thought regardless of your accent or your presentation.

Of course, the structure of your presentation and how you introduce your signposts depends on the purpose of your speech. You'll learn how to adjust these signposts for the ease, comfort and learning of your audience. They'll appreciate you for that.

The final chapter sums up public speaking when English isn't your first language with a series of tips, tricks, and techniques that perhaps no one has thought to tell you. These are "secrets" of the trade, so to speak, that all the great speakers use. Learn as many of these as you can and practice them before your next presentation. When you do this, you'll discover how much smoother your speaking can be.

This small book, as comprehensive as it might be, will never, ever replace the "practice, practice, practice," necessary for you to make the greatest speech of your life. But if you conquer even a few of these techniques, polish up your abilities in a few of the others and embrace the ones that truly talk to you, you're well on your way to making yourself a great speaker. Someone, who in fact, will probably have more invitations to speak in his or her future.

Making the Most of this Book

The key to using this book and to being an effective and popular speaker is to not reading it just once, but making this book a go-to volume whenever you're faced with a speaking engagement. In this way, you can always be sure of brushing up on all the necessary components of public speaking for the ESL student.

Are you ready to prepare yourself for your next speaking assignment? Then I suggest you move on to the next chapter right now.

Chapter 1: Stage Fright Speaks in Every Language, but . . .

Milosh sat at the coffee shop staring at his cappuccino when his friend Raj saw him. Asking if he could sit with him, Raj commented that it looked as if he were deep in thought.

Milosh readily opened up. "English isn't your first language, Raj. You've spoken in public. Weren't you the least bit nervous?"

"But, of course, I was," he said quickly. "Are you scheduled to speak?"

"Yeah, and this is important. If I do a good job, I may be on the shortlist for the promotion at work. No pressure here, right?" He paused, took a sip of coffee and looked his friend in the eye as if asking for advice. Finally, he asked, "How do I survive this, let alone speak coherently enough to win that promotion?"

Have you found yourself in Milosh's position? Do you have nightmares about being in such a position? If you believe it's impossible to present a coherent, well-received public presentation while speaking your second language, English, think again.

You shouldn't be surprised if you experience stage fright when you're invited to speak before an audience – or even to give a presentation to a small group of individuals at work.

Even individuals who have spoken English all their lives know what stage fright feels like. Of course, I understand this innate fear may very well be heightened when English is your second language. I agree, it feels as if that one element throws an entirely new perspective on the event.

But that doesn't mean you can't conquer it. There are some easy ways to overcome stage fright – even when you're speaking in your second language.

In this chapter we investigate the reasons why you – speaking in your second language – may feel the bite of stage fright a bit more than native speakers. We'll even offer you methods that have worked for so many that reduce that fear as much as possible.
Broadly speaking, the fears are formed around five broad concerns.

Fear # 1 – I'm embarrassed by my foreign accent

Many individuals who speak English as a second language have that very same fear: What about my foreign accent? This fear not only includes a general embarrassment of your so-called accent, but the potentially devastating effects you mistakenly believe it may have in your presentation.

Let's get one thing straight right now, even the most polished speakers are sometimes misunderstood. I'm not only talking about those who speak English as a second language, but native American speakers can easily be misunderstood in their own language.

Right now, I'm sure you're not really concerned about those whose first language is English. But what if I told you that even one of the most famous non-native English speakers has been misunderstood when giving a presentation.

Even the Dalai Lama can be Misunderstood

Who? The Dalai Lama. Yes, the Tibetan leader was speaking at Brown University. The closed-caption transcriptionist mistook his saying the word "forget" for another, albeit, rather offense swear word, also beginning with the letter "f."

The context in which this happened appeared simple enough, at least on the surface. The great spiritual leader said that if his listeners had found his ideas thought-provoking, to please share them with others. If not, then they could simply "forget." That's not what the transcriptionist heard or typed.

It's unlikely that such a mistake will happen to you. And should it does happen, you can at least take some solace in knowing it's also happened to none other than the Dalai Lama. So now that we've tried to assuage your fears some, let's emphasize that accents shouldn't be embarrassing.

Many individuals will actually spend more time listening to you speak (as long as they can understand you) with your accent than without. There are always those persons who are enthralled listening to the intonation as well as the meaning of the words.
According to some, that wasn't the first time audience members have mistaken his word "forget" for the other, less tolerated (and much less spiritual) word. Have you heard that he has given up talking in English in public? Absolutely not.

So, let's just push that fear right out of your mind. Not that I'm discouraging you from taking measures to reduce your accent. If you feel that would make you a better public speaker, then the moment you know you need to make a public presentation, then, by all means, start practicing exercises that will help overcome your accent.

Fear #2: What if I can't find the right English words for my topic.

This can be a fear you can simply drop in the trash. You'll have absolutely no problems searching for the correct word as long as you keep on practicing your presentation.
This piece of news is nothing new, speakers have known about it for years. The more you've prepared your speech – in essence, work with words – the easier the proper words will pop into your mind.

This doesn't' matter if your first language is Spanish or Italian. Practice the words that surround your area of interest. The more words you can use when you talk, the better your speech will be. While you're searching for one word using a thesaurus or other word will eventually be followed by even more words.

If you know your topic, chances are you won't forget words. Of course, if you do forget an occasional word, it's not the end of the world. Here, again, even native speakers forget words. Recover and move on. Just keep in mind while you're practicing for this event, that the better acquainted you are with your topic, the least likely you are to forget a word.

Many speakers – regardless of their first language – may forget a word or two simply because they're under stress. That's why practicing can help. It will lessen the stress on you, making it far less likely for you to forget a word here or there or even chunks of your presentation.

You can easily understand why adequate preparation can help relieve your stress and in turn make it easier for your mind to recall the words you need whether it's in your native language or not.

There are still two more tricks you can easily put into effect to help practically ensure that you don't forget a word or two. The first is through preparing the "vocabulary" that forms the majority of your presentation and rehearse it continuously. If you know that every topic has "most used" words and phrases, you'll be wise to study them and, specifically, say them out loud as often as you can.

The second trick is to place special emphasis and concentration on the start of your presentation. By this, I don't mean to emphasize the beginning of your speech to the exclusion of the rest of it. The very first few minutes of this speech are critically important to your success. When you start off on the right foot, as they say, the better and easier it'll be for you to develop the rest of your topic.

By emphasizing the beginning of your presentation and nailing it, you'll also increase your self-confidence dramatically.

Fear # 3 – Is my English going to be easily Understood?

It's a natural fear that you believe that some individuals in the audience may not understand your English. If you speak with an accent, you're probably repeating yourself because people didn't quite grasp what you said the first time around.
But, once again (and I'm sure you're getting tired of me saying it) even some native speakers are tough to understand when they get to the podium to speak.

Your audience will find it much easier understanding you, when you structure your presentation properly, that is, in a logical progression. This ensures that those listening to the speech will be able to follow the flow of your presentation with ease. When it flows, your audience doesn't need to fumble around spending time thinking about how to piece your information together. That gives them more time to listen and comprehend you.

We'll talk more about structure in a later chapter. The way in which you structure your presentation depends on its goal. You'll prepare and structure your talk differently for different messages. This will help your audience in understanding you.

Secondly, much of what we call communication is simply the use of intonation of the language. Your audience is not only listening to what words you say, but also how you say them. A sure way to get their attention – and keep it – is to sound expressive as well as friendly.

Sounding "expressive" really shouldn't be much of a problem. If you're giving a presentation, it's probably about a topic you're at least interested in, if not passionate about. If you can convey your enthusiasm for the topic, then that will filter through to your audience and they'll be enthusiastic too.

More than that, though, your intonation also reflects how your audience perceives the meaning of your words. The identical sentence, spoken with different emphases on different words, can and does take on different meanings.

Here's a quick example of what I mean. Think of the sentence: "I'm sure he'll think of a better plan."

When no one word is stressed above any other it's just a general statement. It carries no implications or connotations.

Now, say that same sentence only emphasize the word "better." This hints that that first plan was less than good.

If you say it emphasizing "he'll" in the sentence, then that implies he is critical of the first plan and may not have even been the creator of it.

When the word "sure" is stressed when you're expressing the fact that there is no doubt in your mind that he can think of a better plan.

As you can see, there are plenty of ways to interpret this sentence depending on the emphasis on your words. Every sentence you speak – especially in your presentation – can be taken and interpreted in a variety of ways, depending on your intonation.

Fear # 4 – I'm afraid my presentation will be boring because I speak too slowly

If this is your fear, you'll be surprised to learn it's really your strength. That's right!

You're aware that it's natural for you to speak in your second language more slowly than you speak in your native tongue. But up to this point, you may have considered it a weakness. At this very moment, it has now become a strength. Congratulations!

This is one area of using your developing language you don't have to worry about. Native speakers are constantly told to slow down when speaking in public. If there is one major criticism – especially those who aren't used to standing in front of the podium -- it's they speak too fast. Their natural rapidity of speech is then exaggerated due to the stress they feel while they are speaking.

I have a friend whose first language is English. He'll practice his presentation, even timing it, ensuring it's just the right length. He doesn't go over his allotted time and he's provided time for questions and answers.

Do you know what happens when he actually gets in front of the audience? He shaves even more time off the presentation because he talks faster than he's ever done in his practice sessions. He speaks even faster because he's nervous.

When you're speaking in public, you can't use the same flow of words as in a normal, casual conversation. Why? Because your presentation (hopefully) contains new information for the audience to digest. They need the time. If they're still trying to process that last sentence you said while you've already covered three more sentences, you've lost them.

That's not fair to them – they aren't receiving all the information you want them to have – or to you. They're missing out on something important you want to convey and have been practicing. Speak too fast and it's a lose-lose situation for everyone.
The best speakers adjust the pace of their speech. By doing this, they ensure that their listeners totally understand what's being said.

The use of the subtle pauses in your speech also conveys certain meanings and adds emphasis to what you're saying. It works, in fact, very much like intonation does. Let's look at the words in this sentence, "If all of us do our share, we will succeed!"

Read it out loud. It could have any number of meanings when read with little enthusiasm and too quickly. Now see how the entire meaning of the sentence changes when you place pauses in all the right places. "If (pause) all of us (pause) do our share (pause) we will succeed!"

Can you see how the second sentence is stronger than the first?

Fear # 5 – Will I understand the audience's questions?

The question-and-answer portion of a speech generates the most fear for most individuals who speak English as a second language. Why? Because they feel as if they aren't in control. They feel they can't rehearse or prepare for potential questions.
Rest assured, that there are even professional speakers who present in their first language who are also intimidated by this portion of the presentation. Opening the floor up to questions is quite risky. You never know who's about to ask what kind of question.
There really are methods you can use to provide you with the self-confidence you need to get you through this portion of the event.

First, you need to convince your inner fear-monger that you really aren't walking into a lion's den unprepared. That's really the truth. You've undoubtedly prepared quite a while on this presentation. All you need to do is to spend just a little bit more time and anticipate – based on what you're talking about – the potential audience questions.

Take a good, long look at your topic. What parts of the speech are most likely to produce the most questions? This becomes fairly easy if you're presenting any controversial or new ideas. Right away, you can count on someone challenging them or at the very least desiring to learn more about them.

Once you have identified these parts, then you can just about guess off the top of your head what questions you'll be asked. Secondly, keep in mind that you are the expert. Look at you. You're the individual standing at the podium. You're the person talking to the audience. That point should not be lost on you. Trust me, it's not lost on the audience. It means (in case you need reminding) that you know your material very well.

Simply put, if you've prepared every other part of your speech, then you'll be able to handle the question-and-answer session – even if English is your second language.

If your fear, as a speaker of English as a second language, is that you won't understand a question, here are a few strategies you can employ to buy you a bit more time before you answer.

Simply ask the audience member to repeat the question under the pretense that you didn't hear it.

Ask the questioner to clarify what he means. In this way, you'll have another chance to hear the question (from a different angle, perhaps) while you're planning your response.

This brings us to the final question in this part. What if, despite everything, you really don't know the answer to one of the questions? Don't panic. It happens to everyone. Simply admit you don't know the answer, that you've never been confronted with the question before this, but that you certainly would be happy to investigate it further. After all, you may decide to add, you're eager to know the answer as well.

In this chapter, we've talked about preparation as the key to gaining any confidence in public speaking. In the following chapter, we'll provide you with a few of the keys to prepare yourself for your big day.

Chapter 2: Practice your English Before you're scheduled to Present

Mllosh sat at his favorite coffee shop reading his notes. His public speaking engagement was fast approaching and he wanted to be doubly sure that he was prepared.

Some of his friends chided him for taking the event so seriously. "Just relax and be yourself," they told him. "There is something called over-preparedness. You already know the material backward and forward, inside and out. What more can you do?"

Milosh, the wise man that he is, ignored this advice. No one needed to tell him he was an expert in this area. That aspect of his public speaking engagement gave him little concern. The part that kept him up at night, figuratively speaking, was the actual speaking.

You've probably have heard this particular advice over and over again. I'm betting you've been told this so much that its full implications may not even register with you much anymore.

It comes to you in two words: be confident. Not only will your friends and family tell you this, but go to any website on public speaking and they'll tell you the same thing. Self-confidence is the key to a speech well presented.

Unfortunately, few of these well-intended people and sites actually tell you how you gain this self-confidence.

Sure some of them start out by saying, "act as if" you already have it and it will eventually settle on your shoulder like a butterfly.

Excuse me, since I've never had a butterfly settle on my shoulder, I'm not sure I'm going to depend on this method. Sure, I can act as if, but I sure hope I have something else in my pocket to bolster my confidence.

What many people don't tell you is that you need to be thoroughly prepared in order to gain that elusive self-confidence.

It's true. The more you prepare, the more self-confidence you'll gain. So instead of lecturing you on the fact that you should have self-confidence like it's a commodity you can go to the corner store and buy off the shelf, I'm going to provide you with a few tips on how you can thoroughly prepare for your public speaking engagement. If you follow and practice these even occasionally, you'll find your self-confidence about talking in your second language grow.

No Time Like the Present.

This is a politely subtle way of saying "this is not a time to procrastinate."

Indeed, it isn't. When should you start preparing for your engagement? If your answer is the moment you're assigned or invited, then you get a gold star. You're absolutely right.

Waiting until the last minute to prepare a speech may work for some people. But it seldom works for those who are presenting in a second language. Allow yourself as much time as possible to prepare.

In fact, it isn't that outrageous of an idea to give yourself an extra week – even two – if you can to focus on this presentation.

Don't Trust Your Memory to Speak Off the Cuff

You may have noticed that some individuals have the talent of speaking extemporaneously. Just jumping off on the spur of the notice and presenting a perfectly structured, finely delivered speech. Or so it may seem so to the audience.

It's true. Some individuals can do this, but more often than not, somewhere along the line, these people have been planning this moment. Sure, they probably weren't scheduled, but in their minds they've probably rehearsed what they would say if they ever got the chance to speak.

Not only that, but they've probably been practicing their English skills as well, in hopes of one day being able to speak in this manner. What appears to be unplanned and off the cuff was probably months in the making.

Write the Speech Out in English.

No, you won't read your speech from your notes, but there are so many advantages to writing it out. First and foremost, the simple act of writing it out will clarify your thoughts.

If you opt to write it in your native language and translate it, you may find that, upon translation, may lead to improper sentence structure as well as some poor phrasing.

Read Your Speech Out Loud

Once you've written your speech, then it's time to read it out loud. This will help you feel more comfortable with the pronunciation of words that may give you a difficult time. This also is valuable in listening to the proper sentence structure of these ideas in English.

And by the way, read it more than once. Reading it more than once provides you with the familiarity you'll need in order to give a first-class, professional style. But more than that, this form of preparedness will give you the confidence you probably never knew you had.

Create a Set of Notes based on your Speech.

Yes. You read that correctly. Once you've written the speech out and read it a few times, then you'll want to take notes on it. These don't have to be extensive notes. They can be fairly simple – enough even to give you a hint of where you're going next in the presentation. If you even create an outline, you'll find this to be of great help. These notes should not be written out in full sentences as much as you think that method would be better.

Instead, the purpose of these notes is to help you keep track of where you are in your presentation as well as where you're headed. If you write out full sentences instead, you may discover this method awkward when you consult them.

Practice Presenting your Speech

Did you really think I would neglect to tell you this? This is one of the most important steps to preparedness. In fact, the ultimate practice session is to give this presentation to a native-speaking friend or two.

This may go without saying, but I'll say it anyway, the more often you can give these practice presentations, the better your presentation will be. In turn, you'll find yourself gaining self-confidence not only in your trial runs, but when you eventually stand in front of that audience.

There is a key to this suggestion, though. Many individuals read their speech in front of friends and family who tell them how great it is. Before your trial run, explain to your "beta listeners" that you want feedback – honest feedback.

Of course, we all want positive feedback, but not at the expense of the quality of our speech. Explain to your listeners that you want – indeed – need their honest criticism. Promise them you won't take it personally. Then, don't take it personally. Instead, think about the reason for constructive criticism for what it's meant to be– a means to make you a better speaker of English.

Record your Presentation during your Practice Sessions

This is critical in truly learning how you sound when you speak in public. Your first thought upon hearing this is to simply record your voice. Give consideration, though, to actually videotaping yourself as well. When you do this, you may find your body language is less than inviting. Or it could be that your body language or posture doesn't match with what you're saying.

You'll also discover when you do this, you may become your worse critic. Take your own criticism with a grain of salt. Sure, you may never get to the level of perfection that you desire, but that doesn't mean you should give up. It may just mean, for one thing, that you're expecting a bit too much from yourself at the moment.

Remember, too, that you've started earlier in preparing than most people just because you know it's going to take you a bit longer to get yourself to the point where you're satisfied.

Reverse Accent Mimicry

Many speakers who present in their second language tend to worry about their accent. English has a few sounds which no other language has – perhaps some of these sounds are new to you. On top of that, though, when you speak English you may become confused by the stress or emphasis of syllables within the words. This is exactly where reverse accent mimicry can help you overcome these hurdles that so many ESL students seem to stumble over.

It could be that right now, knowing you have a speaking engagement in your future, you're concerned about how your listeners will accept and understand your accent.
The concept behind this practice is easy enough. The method simply involves analyzing an English speaker who has a strong English accent speaking in your language. If Spanish is your first language, for example, then you're o searching for someone who speaks Spanish with a thick American accent.

What you're going to do is to speak your native language, in this case, Spanish, as your model is speaking it. Be sure to imitate everything – and I mean everything – the person is saying and how he is saying it. Incorporate all his "mistakes" from difficulties in pronunciation to the grammar issues and the structural difficulties.

The problems that this person has when speaking your language, can reversibly reflect the problems that you will have when speaking English.

When you do this, you'll discover, much to your surprise, that this is a quantum leap in perfecting your own English pronunciation and reducing your accent.

Practice. Record, repeat. Review.

Ask any language instructor. The best way to become fluent in a language is to use it – as often as possible. So it should come as no surprise to learn that by reading your presentation out loud, recording it, then listening to is one of the quickest and easiest ways to become proficient at delivering your speech.

Not only that, but the instructions for doing so, are as simple as reading the instructions on a bottle of shampoo: lather, rinse, repeat. In this case, practice, record, repeat, and review. You've no doubt taken more than enough courses in the English language that these instructions are a well-worn mantra. But just because it isn't a creative approach to practicing for your big day, doesn't mean it's not an effective one. Because it certainly is. In fact, it's one of the most effective, despite its mundane and tedious application.

When you're using this method for your presentation, you simply record yourself reading or better yet, presenting it from your outline without notes – and then listen to the recording. While you should be critical, don't be overly so. Choose one or two areas you'd like to improve in initially and study these diligently. See how many items you can improve upon in the time you have.

Do this until your comfortable presenting your speech, not only the material itself and the outline, but also the intonation of your voice and the stress you place on the syllables of your words and the pauses among your words themselves.

Alternate your Practice Material

But you can take this form of rehearsal one step further. Because inevitably your presentation will become routine for you, alternate reading and repeating your speech with reading other materials. You may want to read a novel, using all the forms of emotion the author intended for the characters to possess.

Do everything you did with your speech, but just practice it with the book. This will keep you speaking English and not boring yourself or sliding into bad habits because you've read your material too many times. Choose a book you've been longing to read and this should keep your interest for a while. In fact, if you choose your reading material wisely, it won't seem the least bit tedious, it may even become a pleasure.

Of course, your selection of exactly what to read out loud and how you do this are only limited by your own imagination. Below are some materials as well as ways to institute this practice if reading novels get boring.

Are you a news hound or a political junkie? Then why not try reading a newspaper or even a website devoted to news or politics. Select a story in a printed newspaper or magazine or one on a website. Read it out loud recording yourself as you go along. Play the recording back, listening to yourself critically. Then record yourself again, searching for ways to improve your speaking.
Do this at least once a day once you've been assigned or committed yourself to the public speaking engagement. This is a form of rehearsal you can easily start even before you've written your speech simply by reading books, magazines, newspapers as well as websites out loud.

Once you begin composing your speech, you then can record snippets of the speech, listen to yourself – and to the actual writing – and know how you sound and, as an added bonus, how well your speech is written.

If you've given yourself the two-week practice time as we've suggested earlier, you'll have plenty of time to correct any words that may be tripping you up. So, there's no need to get frustrated or worried.

Listen to Four Areas

As you listen with an ear to improve your speaking voice, there are four areas in particular that are critical. They're listed below:

Pronunciation and Enunciation

You may think that this goes without saying, but when you speak in public it's doubly important. For one thing, your first goal is to make it as easy as possible for your audience to understand – and not question – what you've just told them. This means that when you express yourself you place the emphasis on the proper syllable or syllables in the words. I've said it before and I'll say it again. You don't want your audience questioning what you said and entirely missing a chunk of vital information that follows.

Make sure you're not mumbling and that each and every word is pronounced clearly. When you are doing this correctly, you may feel as if your mouth is working overtime, exaggerating the movements of your jaw and lips. Don't worry about that. Record yourself. If your words sound clear when you're listen to them, then you can rest assured your mouth isn't in any exaggerated position.

Projection

I know. I know. You're going to have a microphone to amplify your voice. You really don't need to worry about that. But you do – even with a microphone. When you learn how to project your voice, speaking from your diaphragm, then not only will you sound naturally louder but more authoritative as well.

This means, should any mishap occur with the electronics you will still be able to carry on. Not only that, when you speak louder, people automatically assume you're more knowledgeable about a subject. Any doubts you may have in your own mind about them not taking you as seriously as you wish because of the way you speak English will vanish. And that's always a good thing!

Your use of inflection

You might not be able to provide a good definition off the top of your head of the word inflection, but you know it when you hear it. Let's just say you immediately recognize it when you don't hear inflection.

You've probably sat through enough college lectures in which the professors couldn't or felt they didn't need to utilize this tool. The result? Boring courses in which very few students learned much if anything at all! You were subjected to monotone speakers who had more than one student sleeping and many struggling to stay awake. That's not exactly the reaction you want from your audience, now is it?

Instead, you want to make your presentation as entertaining and engaging as possible. And before you say that it's impossible with your topic, think about the TED talks that have become increasingly popular thanks to YouTube and NPR or National Public Radio.

What does TED stand for? Technology, Entertainment, and Design. Notice that the "E" stands for entertainment – not education. While it's a given your presentation will educate your audience, consider that in order to maintain their attention, it should also entertain. Part of the way in which to do this is through a vivid presentation. And that definitely involves the inflection of your voice.

Listening to your Cadence

You've no doubt heard the word cadence before as well. Sometimes it's used when individuals talk about the pace of soldiers walking together. While we're talking words, the meaning is similar. When I mention cadence, I'm referring to the pace of your delivery. Just like you can bore your audience without using varying degrees of inflection, you can do the same with your cadence – or lack thereof.

Listen to your presentation paying strict attention to the speed of your delivery. Is every sentence spoken at the same pace? Is it excruciating slow or do you quicken the pace every now and then based on the emotion you're conveying and on the content of your presentation?

When you can show what you say at critical points you want to emphasize and want the audience to truly comprehend, you can feel comfortable they've received the message. By the same token, if you're telling a story involved in your topic, you might want to speed your pace or cadence to indicate a higher degree of excitement. Again, this is where the TED talks are one of the best examples around of this.

Pauses

A well-defined pause is as important in a talk as the use of any other form of communication. Pauses, when positioned correctly, can build tension if you like (watch any television reality show to confirm this) and to allow your audience to really concentrate on what you've just said.

They're also critical if you've added humor to your speech. A well-timed pause will give your listeners the time to laugh without worrying that they're missing something you've just said.

Chapter 3: Don't Underestimate the Power of Visual Aids

The day of the presentation was fast approaching. Milosh had mixed emotions. He felt excited because he finally gets his chance to speak to his colleagues as well as his supervisors. This is his big break to show everyone how talented he is. He knows if he can perform well on this project his prospects of receiving the promotion he hungers for are greatly increased.

To ensure that the audience fully understands the points he's making, he had decided, upon the advice of a good and trusted friend, to use some equipment to help illustrate his points.

Have you ever heard the adage *a picture is worth a thousand words?*

I'm not sure exactly how many words a picture may actually take the place of, but it's certainly is a near instantaneous way of getting individuals to take notice of the issue at hand. Sometimes merely reciting statistics and stating summaries, while fine, don't drive the issue home like the same facts and figures in illustrated form, from bar graphs to pie charts to photos of economically poor conditions or even natural disasters.

Yes. I know technically this is not a matter of how well you speak the English language. At least on the surface. However, if you dig a bit deeper, below your understanding of the English vocabulary and below your accent, you'll find that equipment you can use to help illustrate your point is priceless.

If anyone in the audience is having difficulty following your speech, you can ensure that the problem will be lessened and most probably eliminated by illustrations. The success of these illustrations, though, are tied to several things. First, you've got to know what equipment is available to you.

Second, you need to know how to use them. I'll just give you a hint. This means learning how to use a PowerPoint presentation properly or slides expertly takes longer than one evening.

In other words, you'll want to start checking out the proper use of these wonderfully inventive and critically useful pieces of technology – perhaps several hours after you've learned about the scheduling of your opportunity. If you're not quite sure what technology, then this chapter gives you a heads up on the most popular and easiest to use aids.

If you're an old pro at using the gadgets, so much the better. You've already been convinced how powerful the addition of these visual aid media can be. If you're not particularly familiar with them, then you may want to ask individuals who have used them. Get their opinions about these aids.

- **PowerPoint presentations**

Without a doubt, a presentation which includes PowerPoint is one of the most engaging, most vital and helpful ways to illustrate ever invented. PowerPoint is a Microsoft software program that makes it easy to create attractive slides to help speakers like you illustrate and illuminate vital points to highlight their importance.

The key to this instantly recognizable electronic slide presentation is to keep any font size you're using large enough to be seen with ease the length of the room. In that way, these slides reinforce what you're already telling the audience.

Many use these to emphasize a point or to add to the content of the presentation through bullet-point summaries of sections of their speech. This is great, but you can do so much more with these as well, including photos of places or screenshots of computer pages. And definitely don't forget to use statistics and charts, as we've mentioned above.

- **Handouts**

No, these aren't particularly technically advanced. But they are still valuable, perhaps more than you can ever imagine. Why? Because the audience can take them home, study them and really learn from them.

Hard copies of pie and bar charts can be crucial to your presentations. Don't dismiss this possibility.

I've attended many presentations and workshops and, unfortunately, don't seem to receive enough of them.

- **Flip charts and markers**

The old-fashioned paper flip chart is still marvelously priceless in some situations. If you're like me, you have the habit of writing while you're talking. In this way, your audience sees the development of an idea or a project.

Flip charts are especially vital if you're inviting the audience to join you in creating a mind map of an idea or concept. It's also a great aid if you're presenting your outline in the mind map form. Not only can you show your thought process clearly, you can use an occasional hand-drawn illustration to emphasize an idea.

You may even discover that one day you'll be brave and confident enough to use different colors on your flip chart.

You'll be amazed how much more clearly your presentation will be received through merely using one of these alternatives, if appropriate. Keep in mind though that especially with any presentation involving computers, there's always a chance that something could go wrong and you'll find that it's not available.

That's the moment you'll be thankful for the backup plan you've devised. If you have PowerPoint slides you think are essential, then make hard backup copies of these. If the computer can't display them for whatever reason, simply pull out your hard copies. You'll get points from your supervisors for not panicking and be extra prepared.

Not only that, but even if the Powerpoint slides work flawlessly, you'll have them stashed away and ready to pull out should you get any requests for them. Once again, you're being perceived as prepared. We all know that perception is everything.

In the next chapter, we embrace another technique professional speakers know that you may not how to build rapport with your audience.

In the following chapter, you'll discover how to win an audience and have them rooting for your success. It's so much easier than you ever thought possible.

Chapter 4: Build a Rapport with your Audience

Milosh felt prepared for his presentation. He had listened to himself more than several times, rehearsed his presentation as well as practicing it in the presence of friends who provided him with useful constructive criticism.

He felt his accent was less pronounced than ever before and in the process of writing his speech, he made sure he knew his topics jargon, but what he felt was even more important, able to translate that into an everyday language his audience could understand.

And he had gone the extra mile, as advised, to produce slides and back up handouts in case the computer plan failed or someone wanted hard copies to take away.

Yup! He felt thoroughly prepared. Then it happened. Someone asked him if he knew how vital it was to create a rapport with his listeners. He hadn't thought of that.

Even though Milosh had a moment of panic, he soon calmed himself down and did a bit of research on how to do that. He thought it was very fortunate he had started working on his presentation early enough to discover how to convince the audience to be on his side.

All the best professional motivational speakers know a tip that they all too often fail to share with other speakers who are beginning their speaking career.

Whether you're planning on making presentations a career or you're only when speaking in public when pushed, it's a secret that you should learn right now: it's essential you learn how to build a rapport with your listeners.

Granted, this is essential for every speaker. But for those who speak English as a second language and those who may be speaking with an accent, this is especially vital. This could mean the difference between gaining the acceptance of those listening to you or to have them sitting in front of you criticizing not only your every move, but also your every use of inflection.

There are basically seven easy ways you can build nearly an instant rapport with an audience – even if you feel they're a hostile group of people when you step on the stage or in front of the podium.

1. Be your own "warm-up" act.

What do I mean by this? Talk to people before your presentation begins. This may mean walking through the aisle, if you're located in a larger auditorium type space or if the group is smaller sitting around with them chatting with a cup of coffee or tea in your hand.

Either way, breaking the ice, so to speak, before you begin your talk really does work wonders when you're a presenter.

This works for those who speak English as their first language, but it also is vitally important if English is your second language. It gives your audience a "preview" of your accent and how to pronounce your words. While you chatting, they'll be processing – whether they realize it or not – the way you speak.

During your "warm-up act" your audience is also getting to know you better, not only personally but also gauging your professional expertise. It's more difficult to be hypercritical of someone they already have made some conversation with than some who are standing in silence or pacing with worry.

2. Ensure your speech and your intentions promote your audience's best interests – and not yours.

If this sentence is a bit vague or fuzzy when you first hear it, but if you allow the meaning to sink in for a moment or two, that light bulb above your head will switch on.

We both know that this presentation is vital to your future. But have you ever stopped to think why these individuals are listening to you? Perhaps this very information you have is vital to them? Have you ever thought they're attending today to improve their future, guarantee their promotion?

If you haven't, think about it. Then do everything in your power to help them understand and digest this material and make it their own. They will be grateful to you.

In other words, you can have two choices once you stand up there and start presenting your material. You can either use this time to "sell" them on some topic or you can view your talk as an opportunity to serve them.

Believe it or not, your audience will recognize the difference immediately. They'll know once you start talking whether you're sincere in "serving" them or you're just paying lip service to that idea. On the other hand, your listeners are no doubt sophisticated enough to know when some are only out to sell them something, whether they need it or not.

How do you want to be remembered? As someone who helped another along their own path, or the individual who tried to hard-sell them?

3. Look audience members in the eye.

If you're fearful of standing at the podium and talking to your audience, you may be tempted to look at the wall behind your audience. I did this at one time. I had hoped the audience would think I was looking at them. In reality, I was only fooling myself.

You really need to take the bull by the horns – or in this case the stage fright by the fear – and look your audience in the eye. By this, I don't mean a quick glance stage right and then a quick glance stage left.

No, choose someone seated in front of you and look him or her straight in the eye. Do this for a few moments, perhaps while you're making a specific or important point, then move on to another individual.

This isn't as easy as it sounds. As you do this you'll also have to know where you are in your presentation. If you're following a mind-map outline you've already revealed for your audience's viewing it becomes easier. You're far less likely to lose your place in your speech.

Eye contact is vital to building a quick rapport. Give it a try. Not only will your audience feel it, and be more willing to forgive you for any deviations in your speaking that results from your accent or your searching for the right word. But, you'll also feel it nearly immediately and you'll feel much more at ease.

4. Approach your topic from your audience's perspective

This tip 's vastly similar to the previous one about "serving" your audience. Of course, your immediate, personal goal is to get through with this presentation in one piece. And hopefully in a manner that may even put you on a short list for a promotion or help your standing at work.

But your long-term is it to address the concerns of your listeners. If you're all colleagues and you're working on a project, then you know either intuitively or because you've talked to them individually about this topic, exactly what their concerns are.

If you're speaking before a group of people with whom you're not familiar, then you're probably presenting materials we all grapple with. Show them you understand exactly what they're going through. They'll appreciate your concern and your ability to help them deal with these concerns.

5. Avoid using language that may offend your audience.

This may seem like a no-brainer. However, as a student of English as a second language, there still may be a few words that trip you up. Some words can be taken the wrong way, some of which may be sexually or racially charged.

This is why it's extremely important for you to have someone you trust to listen to your presentation. If they don't say anything about double-entendres embedded in your presentation, then ask them outright. Better to double check your wording than to make a major faux pas.

6. Interweave stories throughout your presentation.

Humans seem to love to listen to stories and storytellers. I believe it's somehow embedded in our DNA. You'll build a lasting rapport with your audience that will bond you. But more than that, the audience will remember what you've said and it's important because you've linked it with a story they're able to relate to.

7. Be sure your body language says what you intend it to say

Always keep in mind that as the person who is informing your audience, you are the established authority in their eyes. This is true whether it's a group of strangers that you're speaking to and you're not sure of the level of their understanding or if you're giving a presentation to your supervisors.

You might not believe the latter statement, but it's true. At this moment you probably have more current information regarding the subject than your supervisor has. Otherwise, he would be the person giving the presentation.

This means that, first and foremost, your posture needs to speak volumes about you. You need to stand or sit so you have an immediate command presence in the room. You've probably already figured out slouching, legs crossed and other positions which say "I really don't care" are not appropriate at this time.

Additionally, your audience immediately believes, upon seeing this, that you aren't being sincere with them. When that happens, they will no longer accept or maybe even listen to it anymore.

Not quite sure what your body is saying about you? Then have a friend (the one you can trust, of course!) evaluate your body language. Sit or stand as you would giving the presentation. You can even do a dry run of the speech.

Here's an even better idea. Have someone record you while you're rehearsing your presentation. Then you study it. Are there areas in which your body language isn't conveying what you want it to? Could you stand taller or be more poised at places throughout the presentation?

After you view it once, take those movements you believe need polishing and do just that. Decide – perhaps again with a trusted friend – how you can convey confidence or authority in areas in which you seem lacking. Then once you believe you've conquered it record yourself again.

If that sounds like too much work, you may just want to stand in front of a mirror or position a wall mirror so you can view yourself.

In either case, the idea is to discover the best way to use body language to not only impress upon the audience that you're the authority, but that you're open and willing to connect with them as well.

It may seem like a tall order at the moment, but once you begin to practice, you'll see it's much simpler than it sounds.

If you follow these seven tips to building rapport with your audience, you'll discover that building a rapport with your audience is easier than you were led to believe. You'll also discover that the members of the audience will be rooting for you to succeed. And that's always a good feeling.

In the following chapter, you're going to learn how easy it is to make the best use of your language – even if you're giving the talk in your second language, English. Follow me to the next chapter to learn these normally well-guarded secrets.

Chapter 5: Making the Best Use of your Language

Milosh sat once more in his favorite coffee shop deep in thought. His friend walked up to him placed his own coffee cup on the table and sat with him.

"Are you still concentrating on your presentation next week," the friend enquired of him.

When he nodded yes, the friend then asked.

"Is there anything I can do to help you? Anything you want to talk about?"

"My supervisor today," Milosh said, "gave me advice."

"That's great," his friend said enthusiastically. "What kind of advice was it?"

Milosh sighed deeply, answering, "Make the best use of your language?"

"That sounds like good advice," the friend agreed.

"It might be," Milosh conceded, "but I'm not quite sure what it means."

If you're like Milosh, and speak English as your second language it's doubly important that you make the best possible use of your language. There are a variety of ways in which to do this, only a few of which are outlined in this chapter.

Read this chapter over, think about the ways you can use your words to the best possible way – and then do what you believe will make your presentation that much clearer and understandable to your audience's ears.

Speak in Simple Terms

This is no time to show off a big vocabulary, as tempting as it might. Keep any terms referring to your area of expertise as simple as possible so they can be quickly and easily understood.

This is essential advice if English were your native language, but it becomes nothing less than crucial when you're addressing your listeners in a language other than your first.

Your goal as a student of English is to discover the most succinct words and strategically place them in your presentation so your audience automatically knows what you mean. It may mean you find yourself writing your talk more than once in order to select just the right word that denotes exactly what you mean.

Here's is a hint to remember when you're giving a formal presentation. The English language has, at minimum, two different vocabularies. One is the written vocabulary, where you can open yourself up to a wider range of large words.

The other language is our speaking vocabulary. Smaller, simple, easy to understand. This is the one that you ideally want to use when you're giving your presentation. The idea is that you want the audience to spend time on what you're saying not on trying to figure out the meaning of your words.

Clarity

Try not to beat around the bush. Say what you have to say in the fewest amount of terms. If you're not getting your message across, your audience will ask questions at the end of the presentation. If you feel you spent too much time at the end of your talk answering questions that seem to revolve around word use, then perhaps next time you should clarify your language more. The key to this is to file this experience away so you're better prepared for the next time.

You'll also need to take into account who is in your audience. Obviously, if you're presenting to a small group within or corporation who as familiar as you are with the topic, you can expect to sprinkle in some larger words and terms more specific to the industry without the need to explain.

If your audience is composed mostly of lay people who don't have a grasp of the industry jargon, then you'll want to explain events and important facts in smaller, more digestible terms.

The speed of your speech

We've talked about your cadence and pacing earlier in your presentation. This point is closely related. Did you know that the normal pace in giving a presentation – specifically one in which you're trying to persuade someone is between 140 and 160 words per minute?

If you speak any faster than that, you may appear glib and pushy. I knew one gentleman who had been trained as a used-car salesman. I knew it the moment he tried to persuade me to do something his way. His words would come out faster and faster.

It didn't take me long to recognize this. When he started to rev up his speech I simply stopped him and explained to him that nothing he had to say would convince me otherwise, so he could simply save his breath.

We also talked earlier that it was important to speak slowly. But here again, you need to be careful. If you speak too slowly, you may give the impression that you're lecturing them, which in turn, implies that you're "better" than they are. That's not the vibrations you intend to give off at this time.

If you're not sure about how quickly or slowly you're speaking, there's a simple solution. Record yourself for a minute. At the end that minute, count the number of words you spoke. While you're listening to yourself, try to imagine how the audience would interpretation your speed. If you can get inside your listeners head even before you present your speech, you'll be a step ahead and preparation will be much easier.

But more than that, if you speak too slowly your audience will tend to drift off. Keep in mind that the average human ear and brain together can hear, compile and then decode more than 400 spoken words per minute.

The human ear and brain can compile and decode over 400 spoken words per minute, so if you are going too slow your listeners' minds are going to start to wander as the brains find other ways to keep themselves occupied.

Using language to accommodate your audience is essential if you want them to truly understand and appreciate your presentation. If you don't find a way to write and give your speech in a manner that they can understand without sacrificing quality or meaning, then you're really just wasting your time and their time as well.

That would be a shame when, as this chapter shows you, it's so easy to ensure they know exactly what you're talking about and can, in turn, talk about it themselves.

In the following chapter, I'm going to provide you with several ways to help you and your audience know exactly what's coming next in the talk. It's as simple as using words either before or after (or both) a segment of your talk telling them what to expect. The use of what some individuals call transitional phrases and others call signposting.

Why wait any longer trying to figure out what I mean, when you can turn to the chapter right now to begin using these terms and phrases. Not only that proper use of these words will give you a leg up on writing your speech as well.

Chapter 6: Signposting: The Best Kept Secret of Professional Speakers

There he sat, our friend Milosh, who was rewriting his speech. He had written it once already and after reading it out loud, knew something was wrong. But what?

His friend, Raj, agreed to meet him to discuss what was needed. "Nothing, really," Raj said.

Milosh looked at him, not quite believing him. Before he could say a word, though, Raj, explained. "All you really lack are some signposting phrases in order to point your audience in the right direction. Let me show you what I mean. We'll put some in and you'll hear the difference immediately.

Regardless of your first language, signposting is a secret that many professional speakers don't like to reveal to other less experienced speakers. As useful as it is when you're speaking to an audience in your first language, it becomes even more critical to use when English is your second language.

Signposting is surprisingly exactly what it sounds like. It provides your audience with the clues it needs when you're giving them quite a chunk of information at one time.

Using signpost language is nothing more than using certain words and phrases that clue the listener into what is either about to occur in your speech or what you've just gone over.

It's a type of "heads up" to the audience. Those who speak with any type of accent find this quite reassuring that their message hasn't got lost in the midst of their accent.

To explain it in its simplest terms, the use of signposting language actually guides the audience through your presentation. One of the first things you need to know, though, is not using these words generously and to sprinkle them throughout your entire speech.

If you're not familiar with these words, then it's the perfect time to learn them and how to use them.

Start off with the Introduction

That's right! You'll want to start using these vital words in the introduction.

There are several ways you can alert your audience that you're about to tell them what you're talking about today. In introducing the topic and the specific aspects of it, here are popular phrases professional speakers use.

"The topic of my talk today is . . ."

"I'm going to talk to you today about . . ."

"My presentation today is concerned with . . ."

When you're standing up at the podium and you use these words, you'll practically be able to see people immediately paying closer attention to what you're saying. They know you're about to tell them the topic and thesis succinctly.

Giving your Audience an Overview of the Structure of your Speech

The following signpost words are excellent indicators for your listeners. These phrases will help them know in what order you're tackling your topic. You're providing them with clues when you say things like:

"Today, I'm dividing this presentation into four distinct parts . . . "

"I'd like to make seven important points today that are vital . . . "

"Basically, I'm going to be talking about three things today . . ."

"My goal is for you to take three major points away with you today . . ."

"I'll simply start by saying . . ."

"First of all, I'd like to tell you . . ."

"Last of all . . . "

"The next topic we'll cover . . . "

"I would be remiss if I didn't mention . . ."

Finishing a Section

Before you move from one section to another, be sure your audience knows you're done talking about the first. That way there should be little doubt that you've started to talk about another angle of your topic.

You don't need to do this transition with much fanfare. It could be as simple as saying:

"That covers what needs to be said about . . ."

"So far, we've looked at . . ."

When you start a new Section of your Presentation

In the same way that you've provided your audience with clues about where you're taking them in your presentation so far, you can let them know that they're about to start a new section within the speech.

Again this isn't difficult and doesn't take much time from talking about the vital facts. Your listeners will immediately know you're about to take a turn on the road when you prepare them with such phrases as:

We're now moving on to . . ."

"Let's turn our attention to . . ."

"Having said that, the next issue that needs to be covered is . . ."

Analyzing a specific point or providing recommendations

There comes a time in many presentations that you've made your argument or presented the evidence. Your next move then is to inform your audience what you feel it all means. Don't be shy about mentioning to them that they're about to learn what you believe is most important in all of this. They'll know exactly where you're going with this when you use phrases like this . . .

"So, what does all of that mean?"

"Let's look at the evidence in a bit more detail."

"It's time to translate this information into terms that really matter to you . . ."

"Why would we even consider this all important?"

"The significance of all this data is . . ."

Providing the Listener with Examples

You'll also want them to have a few moments before you start dealing with specific examples in your speech. Examples are great ways of illustrating your point and in effect, bringing it to life. You can easily let your audience know you're about to do this through the following language:

"For example . . . "

"A good example of what we've just covered . . ."

"A good illustration of this principle . . ."

"To illustrate this point, I'd . . ."

When it's Time To Conclude

Just as it's important your audience knows when you're taking certain turns in the road of your talk, you also need to give them a heads up when you're getting prepared to conclude.

Before ending your speech, you'll no doubt want to sum up what you've said, wrapping everything up in a nice package for them to take home with them. Below are some very effective reasons you're about to do just that.

"To sum up . . . "

"Let's summarize what we've talked about today"

"If I can just pull this all together for you . . ."

"I'd like to recap what we've covered . . ."

"I'd like to conclude briefly with these words . . ."

"Just to summarize what I've covered in this presentation . . ."

"Just a reminder to the issues we've covered today . . ."

Paraphrasing your Presentation

Many of the most effective speakers not only summarize what they've covered in their talks, but clarify and paraphrase what they've talked about. Again, signposting in this section is easy enough by using transitional phrases such as:

"Simply stated . . ."

"In other words . . ."

"What I'm saying is . . ."

Introducing the question and answer segment

Your next step may very well be to welcome questions from the audience. There's no reason to approach this in an awkward manner. You can easily slip into this section simply by using any of the following phrases:

"I'd be happy to answer any questions at this time."

"I'm willing to take questions from the floor at this time."

"Does anyone have any questions?"

"Please feel free to ask any questions you may have."

"Can I answer any of your questions at this time?

These are just a few of the ways you can use signposting to help guide your audience. While many native speakers seem to know how to use these transition phrases naturally, sometimes those who speak English as a second language need reminding.

Not only that, if you're fearful your audience isn't following along due to your accent, this gives them a chance to catch up to you and reflect on what you've been saying.

In the next chapter, I offer you a few miscellaneous tips that every professional speaker knows in keeping their audience's attention, but seldom share with others. Read the next chapter to get a leg up on other speakers who give presentations in English when it's their second language. It'll ensure your presentation will be well received.

Chapter 7: Miscellaneous Tips

Four, three, two . . .

Milosh was on the final countdown of his formal presentation.
He had everything aligned as best he could. His friend found
him in his office muttering. When Raj realized Milosh was
spending one or two last times reading over his presentation,
Raj apologized. He explained he merely wanted to give Milosh
this small pamphlet. It was called "Miscellaneous Tips all
Speakers Must Know."

"It's never too late to take a look at a few more tips," he said
cheerily. "And good luck, I'll be rooting for you."

1. Breathe, Baby, Breathe!

Your first and natural response to this advice are probably, "Of
course, I'm breathing! Thank goodness it's one thing I don't
have to worry about." Your body may always be breathing, but
sometimes in times of distress, you breathe a bit shallower
than usual.
Many individuals find themselves standing in front of an
audience about to present their speech in their second
language, is a time of distress. It's at this time you find
yourself telling yourself exactly that, "breath, baby, breath."

In fact, it's exactly at this moment, you'll need to remind
yourself to breathe. So how do you do that?

Before you step in front of your audience, practice this short but effective relaxation technique.

First, stand still. Close your eyes. Envision yourself being suspended from the ceiling with nothing but a thin string holding you.

It's now that you want to actually listen to your breathing. Once you're concentrating on your breathing, then simply count to six while you're inhaling. Count another six breaths while you're exhaling.

If you find this relaxation exercise a bit much to envision – and many do – then instead see yourself on a relaxing beach in the sun. For just a moment, visualize how it would feel to be there. Now count your breaths as you breathe deeply. Six in and six out.
This should help you be more comfortable and in turn more confident in front of your audience.

2. Facing the Dreaded Question and Answer Period

Even speakers whose first language is English very often dread the final question and answer period of a talk. Part of it is the natural fear of the unknown. You, as the speaker, have no idea what kind of questions that may be thrown your way.

It's bad enough when you're concerned if you're going to be able to answer questions intelligently about the material itself. If English is your second language, there's a voice in the back of your mind asking yourself, "Will I be able to use the proper language in answering? Or worse yet, "Will I be able to understand the terms my questioners present me?"

One way to circumvent this, at least for a few moments is to answer the question "provisionally." By this, I mean you can answer the question off the top of your head, but explain to your audience you may revisit that answer again – especially if you discover a better way to phrase it.

If you've understood all the terms and are grappling with a way to answer the question in English you can stall at least momentarily simply by prefacing your answers.

Before giving an answer, use phrases like, "Off the top of my head . . . " or "The first thing that comes to mind is . . ." In this way, your audience knows clearly that your answer is really just a first impression. It gives you a chance to think about it as you go along and change your mind without appearing like you don't know what you're talking about.

If you feel uncomfortable with these prefaces, try saying something a bit more nebulous such as "I'll check to see if this is really true, but . . ." You may even say, "I have the exact figures for that at my office or on my computer . . ." You may also offer to check it out and get back to them.

In this way, you've not only provided a provisional answer but you've gone the extra step of checking out to ensure you've given the proper answer. Believe it or not, that goes a long way to establishing your credibility and your authority.

3. Discover the source of your fears.

As much as I've been saying, you still may not believe it. I'm going to say it one more time, though. It's natural to be nervous and even fearful before giving a presentation or talking in front of a group of people.

The ultimate source of most people's fears is not related so much to the actual presentation as they are to the natural human fear of the unknown. Think about it, you're not fearful of not knowing your topic. My goodness, you're probably one of the most knowledgeable in your area of expertise. It's more than nebulous fear you have that as you stand before that audience you may not be ready for every problem or situation that may occur.

Let's face it, the truth of the matter is that when you do step up to the podium you have, in effect, relinquished control of your future – at least for the next hour or so. Anything, literally anything, could happen.

Before you present, ponder for a moment what exactly you're afraid of. Are you afraid someone judging you when they hear your accent, or commenting rudely on your use of vocabulary?

You don't want to step up to the microphone and allowing that fear grip you. Remember the adage, what you fear most comes to you. In order to perform at your best, you need, then, eliminate your fears. Change the way you think, the way you view your experience and you'll be, in effect, changing the experience itself.

Believe it or not, your fear is something you can easily eliminate and in the process, therefore, virtually assure that you'll succeed.

Here are an extra heads up about what audience is thinking. Overall, those people you're about to talk to really do want you to succeed. Trust me they didn't come to hear you talk with the thought, "Let's see how badly this person is going to do."

Here's another hint. If you are true to yourself and you can talk clearly about your subject matter, you've conquered at least three-quarters of your battle with fear. The rest is smooth sailing.

4. Use the wall push to help banish tension

There are many physical exercises you could use to ease your tension, especially right before you begin your talk. This is the same exercise that Yul Brynner used to ease his stage fright when he starred in "The King and I" on Broadway. If he could face down those theater critics with this technique, then it should work very well for you. Here is all you need to do:

Standing approximately eighteen inches from a wall, place your palms flat on it. Push against the wall. While you do this, your abdominal muscles will contract. When you inhale, be sure you hiss and contract the muscles located just below your rib cage. The overall effect should feel as if you were rowing a boat against the current. You only need to do this a few times and it'll actually banish your stage fright. Really!

5. Experiment – and Have Fun while you're Doing it.

"Impossible," Milosh protested. "How can I even imagine have fun? I'm practically scared to death."

And having fun is just the ticket to help to sweep that fear out of your mind. Instead of being so very serious, make up your mind that you're going to have fun with the audience.

You can do this by finding new, innovative ways to connect with your audience. You may want to try taking a new approach to the material – one that will inject humor in the subject.

You may want to try walking into the audience and just wandering around to various places. Each time you do something different be present enough **to gauge the audience's reaction**. You'll know what they and you enjoy most.

Once you begin to enjoy yourself, you'll feel much less self-conscious about it. You'll find yourself being "in the moment" as they say and before you know it, both you and your listeners will be having a great time – and you'll be getting your message across.

6. Meditate before your presentation.

No, let's set the record straight right now. You do not have to be a monk or even the least bit spiritual to meditate. More business executives than ever before are meditating right now because they've discovered that the time they spend stilling their minds actually is invested greater productivity and more concentration on their tasks at hand.

If they spend twenty minutes in meditation, they may gain at least twenty minutes, thirty or even sixty minutes or more throughout the day. Many executives now go on ten-day meditation retreat programs. You may think that after spending ten days out of the office (ideally total out of reach) that they would return to a mess.

It's true that there is work waiting for them, but they are so refreshed that they can take care of the work in record time.

In your case, even a few minutes – as little as five – sometime the night before or an hour before you present could mean the difference between quivering in your wingtips and sailing through a stress-free talk that everyone enjoys, especially you.

7. Answer questions as they arise.

That's right. Perhaps you've asked the audience to wait until you've finished the presentation to ask questions. But believe it or not, there are always a few people (like myself) who can't seem to wait until the end. Perhaps some of us are intuitive about what's coming up next so we ask questions in the middle of your talk.

Some speakers will politely push the question aside by saying "we'll get to that in a few moments." The best speakers, however, will answer that question, even if they have to adjust the talk accordingly.

Why? For one thing, they realize they have the attention of at least one person. And your talk has interested the person enough that he wants to engage with you. That's awesome! It also deserves encouragement.

But there's also another universal reason to do this. The best presentations should feel like a conversation, just a friendly chat between friends. When you stop the train of thought you're on and answer the person's questions you have the opportunity to create an atmosphere that approximates

If you happen to have a slide or other graphic that illustrates this then skip to that while you're answering the question.

Most of the individuals are worried that especially since English is their second language they may get hopelessly lost if they divert from their intended outline, even a bit.

Don't worry. If you've prepared you'll have absolutely no fears of getting lost. I'm betting that this short detour will only gain the attention of the audience and help to increase your enthusiasm and your overall performance.

Never, ever ignore that chance to encourage interaction between you and your audience. That's really the ultimate goal of your presentation.

Conclusion

Yes, speaking in public strikes fear in the hearts of most of us. In fact, if right now, you're feeling pangs of stage fright at the thought of your upcoming presentation, don't worry. It's normal.

How normal? Statistics show that almost three-quarters of the adult population in North America are afraid facing an audience. It's probably saved to say – even though I have no hard statistics to back me up – that the majority of those individuals are native English speakers. So, if they are fearful, you too can expect to be a bit intimidated by what you're about to do.

Ironically, though that fear keeps few people from giving talks. It's amazing how many speeches are given each year by both professional, non-professional and indeed members of corporate America.

Just look around you. There's no dearth of presentations, talks and motivational speakers. That means that if all of these individuals have overcome their stage fright, you can too.

And one of the quickest way to help build your confidence as an individual who is presenting a talk in English is to ensure your English is as good as it can be. If you're confident in the way you speak if you're confident that your accent is not blocking people from understanding your message and if you're confident that you know your material, then you'll be a huge success.

You may be thinking right about now, that's an overload of ducks to get in a row before the date of your presentation. Once you review what's being asked of you and your own potential, then you're already on the road to recovery from stage fright.

I can't help you learn about your topic. That part is up to you. I have to presume that you're already an expert in your field and you have something important and eye-opening information to provide others.

What I can help you with is to aid in preparing your English language skills, from building a vocabulary to helping you reduce your accent. I'm hoping that this small book will help you in learning the nuances of the English language, how to pronounce words properly, provide the right inflection essential for entertaining and engaging speech making.

All you need to do is to choose the topics, tips and techniques you believe will do you the most good and begin practicing them. This implies that you can't wait until the night before to begin preparing for your big day. Give yourself as much time as you can.

Yes, I know that sometimes events like this are foisted upon you and you don't have the time you'd like to prepare. Whatever time you've been assigned to this event, take it. Embrace it. And use it to your advantage. If you have just learned today that you have a speech to deliver, then start today. Give this book a thorough reading. Put as much time into preparing today as you can. Continue daily to dedicating some effort to it.

In this way, your speech will remain uppermost in your mind. Your efforts in refining your English will turn, much more quickly than you can ever imagine, will bear fruit.

But beyond the tips in this book, you must remember one thing: you have everything within you right this moment to succeed in your assignment. If you keep affirming that, then all your practice and effort will be even more effective than predicted.

As you practice your speech, refine your English and polish your presentation skills, there are other small, but very important things, you can do. What do they include?

Think positively.

Never doubt for a minute that you will succeed. Your own confidence will reflect in your performance. Guaranteed.

Prepare.
That's what this book is all about. Whether you have two weeks, two days or two hours, take as much of this time as you can to prepare. Prepare your presentation. Prepare your English. Prepare your mindset.

Preview

After you've prepared, then preview what you're presenting. Pour your energy and positive thoughts into it.

Relax.

That's right. After you've done everything you possibly can think of – relax. It's not healthy to brood over a possible outcome in the future. Trust that it's all going to be well.

Enjoy.

If you've got to be at the podium giving a presentation, you might as well enjoy it. Remember at this moment, you're at the height of success in your career. Be proud of yourself. You've worked hard to get there. So take your time and enjoy the ride.

Smile.

As you're enjoying yourself, let your audience know that. Smile at them. They'll smile back. But even before you stand before that podium, smile while you're piecing your presentation together. Smile while you work. It may sound silly, but you'll see how much easier preparing can become.

Reward.

Don't forget to reward yourself. Reward yourself when you first discover you've been chosen to present your speech. Reward yourself as you reach your self-imposed milestones. Reward yourself when you've completed your preparation and practice and you're ready to stand in front of that podium to present.

As you complete each of your self-imposed milestones, try to find a creative way to give yourself a pat on the back. If you can afford to go and buy yourself something, then do it. You and you alone know the best way to make yourself feel good. You're accomplishing something good here. Be sure you remind yourself of that.

Gratitude.

That's right! Be grateful that you've been given such an awesome opportunity as this. Be appreciative for the chance to hone your speaking skills in this amazing fashion. Be thankful that starting with this moment, every time you speak, you'll be stronger in your presentation skills, and most importantly, in your ability to speak English will be all that much stronger.

Thank you for reading "Advanced English Collection: 3 Books in 1 Bundle". If you liked this book. Please take a minute to share your thoughts and post a review on Amazon. It'd be greatly appreciated.

Remember: **immersion** *is the key to learn any language. If you find yourself* **thinking** *in English, you are on the right track!*

I wish you the best and good luck!

Whitney Nelson

Made in the USA
Columbia, SC
20 March 2024